Happy Diving

Carl Trepanier

The Vancouver Area Diving Guide

First in a Series of Five Diving Guidebooks
to the B.C. Coast

An incentive to encourage you to visit in summer time! Check out dive # 122. From our front garden you ~~you~~ could throw a rock at the lighthouse and almost hit it !!

Gordon Soules Book Publishers Ltd.
West Vancouver, Canada
Seattle, U.S.

Canadian Cataloguing in Publication Data

Trepanier, Carl, 1963-
The Vancouver area diving guide

ISBN 0-919574-81-5

1. Scuba diving—British Columbia—Vancouver Metropolitan Area—
Guidebooks. 2. Vancouver Metropolitan Area (B.C.)—
Guidebooks. I. Title.
GV840.S78T73   1994   797.2'3'09711   C94-910708-5

Published in Canada by
Gordon Soules Book Publishers Ltd.
1352-B Marine Drive
West Vancouver, BC V7T 1B5

Published in the United States by
Gordon Soules Book Publishers Ltd.
620—1916 Pike Place
Seattle, WA 98101

Front cover photo and marine life photos on back cover by Doug Jeffery
Author's photo by Pierrette Trepanier
Dive site photos by Robert Orr and Carl Trepanier

Cover design by Harry Bardal
Typesetting by A.R. CompuType Graphics, Vancouver, BC, Canada
Printed and bound in Canada by Best Book Manufacturers

This book is respectfully dedicated to the wonder and beauty of the ocean world. In bringing to light some of its magnificence, it is my hope that more people will respect and protect the precious gift granted us here and in oceans everywhere.

Contents

Map of Howe Sound **70**

Part Three: Diving in Howe Sound **71**

Acknowledgments

My most overwhelming debt is owed, without any chance of adequate repayment, to Rob and Mary Orr, who provided computer skills and hardware, photographic and dive buddy services, and their boat, the *Salty Parrot*.

Next, my thanks go to Gordon Soules and his staff for advice and encouragement. Patient and professional, encouraging and enlightening.

Doreen and Doug Jeffery of West Coast Scuba Centre were of great help, providing air, photographs, and dive store contacts.

Thanks to all the dive buddies who ventured out to sites unknown and untested without ever a complaint if we hit a less-than-wonderful area. These folks include Lenny Marriott, Bill Powell, Rob Orr, Maurice Lavoie, Wendy Boehm, James Petrovich, Randy Smith, Peggy Hellyer, Pete Schouten, Phil Gell, Brenda Buckner, Paul Cartmill, Sue Anderson, Ken Hearn, Dwayne Geisbrecht, Deborah Hadath, Rob Rogers, Gord Prothero, Darcy Elder, Annie Storey, Tom Williams, Linda McManus, Ron Schaeffer, Betty Pratt-Johnson, and Sandra Hobbs.

Special thanks to Bill Powell for marine identification tips and the odd boat trip, to Lenny Marriott of L and J Sport Diving for rides and for being a guaranteed dive buddy, and to David Stone of the UASBC for volumes of information on local wrecks.

Thanks to others, including the following, who helped in other ways: J. R. MacDougall, W. S. Crowther, Mel Shyng, and Chris Florek of the Department of Fisheries and Oceans; Susanne Lukas and Bill Farnworth of the Canadian Coast Guard; Lynne Trepanier for superb technical help on maps and charts; Darcy Elder for software and hardware; Thomas Ng for computer graphics assistance; Doug Bencze, Richard Dixon, Sue Madson, Phil Gell, Mike Paris, Ron Stead, Maya Vryheid, Rick Waugh, and Chris Charlton for assistance compiling the dive club listings; Andy Lamb for information on marine identification courses, marine life sanctuaries, and coastal fishes; Scott Stepaniuk for the barge and for info on sites; Gerry Powell and Janet Marriott for boat tending; George Klikach for info on Whiskey Cove; Lisa McIntosh for some marine identification tips; Danny Bereza for his slip in Coal Harbour and for showing some favourite sites; and Mike Flood and Ginny Smith, who took me out diving for fun once in a while.

Thanks to all the divers who, when I brought up the possibility of writing a book, responded with enthusiastic support and encouragement.

No dive guidebook written about an area in B.C. is complete without special thanks to Betty Pratt-Johnson. A person of boundless energy and goodwill, Betty is responsible for bringing the joy and wonder of the underwater world to thousands of people who asked the question "Where can we dive?" Thanks from all divers in the protected waters of Washington and British Columbia.

Finally my thanks to Sandra Hobbs for encouragement, support, love, and enthusiasm, not to mention editing and typing. Your patience and understanding made the difference.

Disclaimer

This book is intended as a guide to dive sites in the Vancouver area. It is not to be used in place of proper dive plans. Divers must evaluate site conditions and suitability for themselves. This book in no way relieves divers of their responsibilities to organize, plan, and execute dives in a safe manner consistent with training and experience levels. Diving is always at your own risk.

This book is not a training manual. It is intended for use by divers with scuba certification from recognized certifying agencies.

Caution

Reproductions of information from Canadian Hydrographic Service charts are for illustrative purposes only; they do not meet the requirements of the Canadian Charts and Publications Regulations and are not to be used for navigation. The appropriate up-to-date charts and the relevant complementary publications required under the Charts and Publications Regulations of the Canada Shipping Act must be used for navigation. See page 21 for information on obtaining Canadian Hydrographic Service Charts.

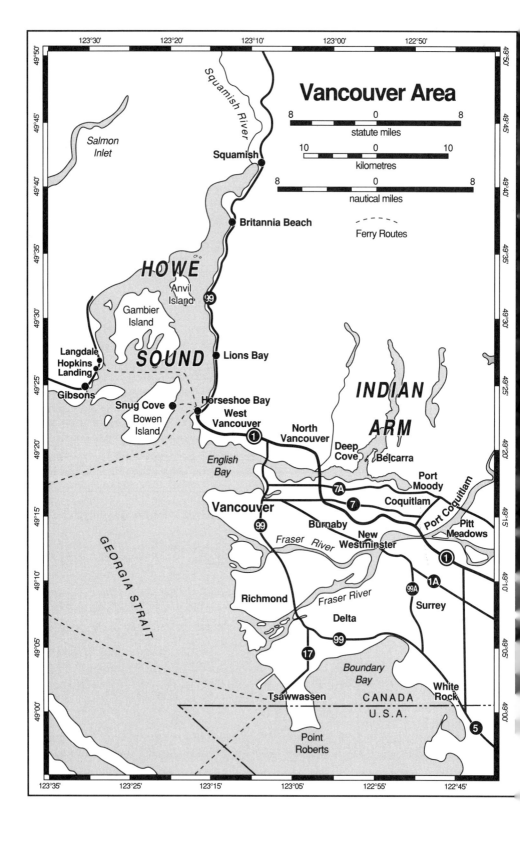

Part One: General Information for Divers

The Vancouver area offers a diverse and exciting world to scuba divers. Vancouver's active diving community and visiting divers enjoy many good sites and services. Vancouver waters are prized for their diverse geography, fascinating marine life, and abundance of opportunities for exploration. There is something for all divers, whether they enjoy night dives, deep dives, wrecks, walls, photography, bottle collecting, or marine life identification. There are two attractive areas for diving in the Vancouver area: Indian Arm to the northeast of the city and Howe Sound to the northwest. Other waters in the Vancouver area, including English Bay and Boundary Bay, lack variety in geography and marine life to make them interesting to most divers or have heavy ship and boat traffic. Diving is not permitted between First and Second Narrows.

Using This Book

NAME OF DIVE SITE   Based on a prominent geographic or underwater feature.

THE DIVE AT A GLANCE   A summary of information found in the site write-up.

SKILL LEVEL   Criteria for assigning skill level ratings are as follows:

Skill level 1.   Easy entry; negligible current; gently sloped shallow bottom, flat bottom, or shallow wall. For divers with entry-level certification.

Skill level 2.   As above, with occasional mild current, a medium-sloped bottom, or a bottom that can go deeper than 60 feet. For divers with some diving experience beyond entry-level training.

Skill level 3.   A site with entry, current, or depth considerations that require advanced skills. For divers with advanced training.

Skill level 4.   A bottom that drops to extreme depths or a strong current. For divers with advanced training and developed skills.

On certain sites, a variety of depths and currents allows groups of mixed abilities to dive different sections of the site. These sites are given multiple skill level ratings. Skill level ratings are given as a guide only. Unforeseen elements may temporarily or permanently change a site. Divers must make a thorough dive plan, taking into account conditions at the site on the day of the dive. Dive only in conditions equal to or better than those in which you have had training or experience, and remember that diving is always at your own risk.

ACCESS   Access to dive sites is by shore, boat, or either shore or boat.

LOCATION   A general placement of the site within Indian Arm or Howe Sound and specific information on roads, landmarks, anchorages, entries, and, in some cases, direction of travel. As the Greater Vancouver area is a growing, changing area, divers should consult an up-to-date road map before venturing out.

HAZARDS   A list of factors that must be taken into account when planning and executing the dive.

Boat traffic: Indian Arm and Howe Sound are popular boating areas. Always fly a dive flag and surface close to it. Listen for the sound of boats when underwater. Look up when surfacing and reach up with one hand when near the surface. There may be times when you have to remain under and allow the traffic to pass, so you should leave the bottom while you still have a reserve of air. Once you are at the surface, take a quick look in all directions. Sailboats are very quiet and just as dangerous as power boats should they run into you. Boats can also cause problems after they have passed through the area. Their wake can create surge in shallow water and make entries and exits difficult. Watch for waves when approaching shore.

Current: Wind and tidal movement can generate current that is strong enough to cause discomfort, fatigue, or loss of directional control. Dive within your experience, and always check local marine weather forecasts and the *Canadian Tide and Current Tables* (see page 21) as part of your dive plan. If you are caught in a current at the surface, make yourself positively buoyant and signal for help. If you feel you must swim, swim across the current rather than into it. Sometimes it is easier to walk along the shore than to fight a current to a desired point. If you are diving from a boat, you can use drag lines or a live (tended) boat. Start your dive into the current; it is much easier to drift a short way back than to battle the current over a long distance.

Depth: At some sites, depths fall away very quickly. At other sites, no bottom is visible. Always maintain proper buoyancy control, positive at the surface and neutral under the surface; carry depth and pressure gauges and refer to them frequently; and, whenever practical, use a descent/ascent line.

Fishing line: Many good dive sites are also popular fishing sites. Entanglement in fishing line is rare, but divers should carry a knife and be alert for line draped on the bottom.

Red jellyfish: Usually a summer/fall hazard. Some jellyfish trail up to 25 feet of tentacles, which, even if they are separated from the animal, can impart a nasty sting on exposed skin. Divers should have their buddies check for tentacles before removing equipment and keep a sting neutralizer in their first aid kits.

Visibility: Fresh water runoff, algae blooms, wind, low light, and careless stirring of the bottom by fins can reduce visibility to "faceplate vis" and cause disorientation. Lights, compasses, depth gauges, reference lines, and proper buoyancy control help divers cope with limited visibility.

Wind: Wind can generate a number of problems for divers. On the surface, wind can cause waves and swell sufficient to make shore entry and exit difficult or impossible and boat rides, entries, and exits uncomfortable or dangerous. Dive buddies can become separated and have difficulty reuniting if high waves obscure their view. Wind-generated surface current can cause discomfort or loss of directional control, forcing divers towards rocks or shores and away from their objective. Even at seemingly calm sites, swells caused by wind many kilometres away can make diving challenging or unsafe. Underwater surge and obscured visibility are often the results of wind action on the surface. The best way to deal with wind is to collect information from weather forecasts and evaluate conditions before suiting up or heading out. Marine weather broadcasts are available on VHF Radio Channels WX 1,2, and 3 and 21B. They can also be heard by telephone by dialing (604) 270-7411.

Please note: The methods listed above may not deal adequately with all hazards at all times. Divers who are uncomfortable or nervous with conditions should consider aborting the dive. The ocean has been around for millions of years and will wait for your return. Aborting a dive is a sign of maturity and good judgment.

DESCRIPTION A short description of the site, including geography, bottom type(s), depths, and marine life. Since most depth gauges sold in British Columbia measure depth in feet of water at sea level, this is the measurement used in this book. In most descriptions, depths are given in the first paragraph. In descriptions of sites with complex bottoms, depths are included as part of the narrative of the site.

WHEELCHAIR ACCESS This section expands on the information given in the access and location sections of all shore dives and covers the needs of disabled divers with regard to entering the water from the shore. Boat dives are accessible to disabled divers depending on their skill level and experience.

PHOTOGRAPHS AND CHARTS A photograph of the entry point and a note giving the perspective of the photograph to help divers orient themselves. A nautical chart extract gives the site's general location.

MEASUREMENTS Water depths are measured in feet of sea water. Distances on land are measured in kilometres. Marine distances are measured in kilometres and nautical miles.

Further Information for Making Dive Plans

ENVIRONMENTAL CONDITIONS Divers must evaluate conditions at the site before entering the water. Factors such as bottom type, depths, surface and subsurface temperatures, tide and current movement, visibility, and wind should be considered when making a dive plan. A brief description of these factors as they affect diving in Indian Arm and Howe Sound is given in this section as a general guideline only. Specific plans for specific sites and days should take into account seasonal variations and use up-to-date information, which can be obtained from the sources given in this section.

Bottom type: In Indian Arm and Howe Sound, the site bottom can be a single type or a combination of types including sand, silt, mud, rock, and boulder. Bottoms may be flat, gently sloped, medium sloped, steep sloped, or sheer wall. Pinnacles and islands may contain a number of different arrangements. Crevices, fissures, overhangs, and small caverns are also possible. Divers who are having difficulty with buoyancy control should avoid bottoms that are easily stirred or that slope away at steep angles or as walls.

Surface and subsurface temperatures: In Indian Arm and Howe Sound, temperatures above and below the water are greatly affected by seasonal variations. Surface temperatures also depend on the time of day, and underwater temperatures vary with depth.

Surface temperatures can range from below zero Celsius to 30 degrees or more above zero. Add the sun and the influence of wind, and the fluctuations are, at times, incredible. It is important to bring the proper protection for the entire range of temperatures you are likely to encounter. Think of your needs for before and after the dive. Extra clothing can always be removed, but forgotten items are impossible to don. When gearing up, make sure you do not expose yourself to prolonged heat or cold while readying gear or moving to the site.

Subsurface temperatures play an important role in determining the amount of exposure protection divers wear while under water. Water temperatures in all but the very top few feet of water seldom move above 20 degrees Celsius, so 6-millimetre wetsuits, boots, gloves, and hoods are considered minimal thermal protection. During summer months, temperatures average from 8 to 15 degrees Celsius with noticeable thermoclines. In winter months, the temperature normally averages 5 to 8 degrees Celsius but can drop to as low as 3 or 4. Wetsuits are comfortable attire for some divers even during these cold snaps. Drysuit divers, though, have more protection against cold water. Divers using either type of suit should be alert for signs of hypothermia and should leave the water and warm up before they feel cold.

Tide and current movement: Tidal movements can change the way a dive site looks underwater and on the surface. With tides as high as 17 feet, above-water references and underwater attractions can appear at different levels depending on the height of tide. Large tidal exchanges affect visibility at some sites. Water movement in and out of some areas loosens the bottom and drags particles of silt, obscuring visibility. Tidal predictions for the Vancouver area are found in the Department of Fisheries and Oceans publication *Canadian Tide and Current Tables*, volume 5. For Indian Arm, the reference port is Vancouver, with corrections for height and time given for Port Moody and Deep Cove. Divers in Howe Sound use Point Atkinson as the reference port, with corrections given for Gibsons and Squamish.

Current movement in Indian Arm and Howe Sound is less predictable than tidal movement. Since there are no confined narrow channels to funnel moving water through, no current stations are established in either the Arm or the Sound. Currents can run up to 1.5 to 2 knots in some areas, most notably between Whytecliff Park and Lookout Point in Howe Sound and around Hamber Island in Indian Arm. The best method of predicting current is to look at the tidal exchanges for the area you plan to dive. Quick changes involving large height differences usually mean that divers can expect some current activity. On boat dives, a tender in the boat solves any problems the current may cause.

A working knowledge of the *Tide and Current Tables* is essential for all divers. The tables' introductory section explains how to read them and how to make different calculations based on the information supplied. Sailing and boating courses also teach how to use the tables. See page 21 for further information.

Visibility: There is a great range of visibility in the Vancouver area. Seasonal variations and weather can reduce vision to 5 feet or less. Crisp winter days can give miraculous 100-foot visibility. Generally summer is the murkiest season. Algae blooms reduce visibility for three to five weeks around both April and August. Fresh water input from the Indian River, the Buntzen Power Plant and many creeks and streams affects Indian Arm. Fresh water, silt, and pollution from the Fraser River and the Squamish River reduce visibility in Howe Sound. In summer, visibility in the Arm and the Sound averages about 10 to 20 feet and on very clear days reaches 60 feet or more. In winter, the water is clearer; visibility averages 20 to 30 feet and on exceptional days reaches 100 feet. Localized pockets of poor visibility can be caused by tidal movement carrying silt and debris and prolonged rains running down mountainsides or through culverts into isolated spots. Wind action can also generate sufficient surge and water movement to cloud shallow water. Other localized incidents of poor visibility can be attributed to divers with bad buoyancy control and fin technique.

Wind: Both Indian Arm and Howe Sound are long, narrow stretches of water framed by high mountains. Winds tend to funnel through the mountains in southerly outflow or northerly inflow directions. Usually the outflow is in the morning and the inflow in the evening. Southern Howe Sound with its wider spaces is subject to winds from all directions. Winds in both areas tend to be strongest during the winter months. Gusts of 60 knots or more have occurred during storms in both areas. On most days, though, the wind tends to be from 5 to 15 knots. Winds of 15 to 20 knots usually cause problems for boat divers and shore divers at sites that face the wind.

Wind prediction in Indian Arm is sometimes difficult. There are no weather stations reporting from the Arm, and it is not easily visible from Vancouver. Divers should check the local forecast and make a determination once in the area. Howe Sound has its own forecast on the Marine Weather Channel. It is broadcast continuously on VHF Radio Channels 21B and WX 1,2, and 3 and can be heard by telephone by dialing (604) 270-7411. Updated wind and wave conditions are given for Point Atkinson. Pam Rocks automated station gives wind and barometer readings, which are also broadcast on the weather channel.

EMERGENCY CONTACT INFORMATION   The Greater Vancouver region's emergency telephone number for ambulance, police and fire is 911. If calling about a diving-related accident involving the use of compressed air, be sure to inform emergency personnel that they are responding to a scuba diving emergency. Be ready with location and details of the accident.

Marine emergencies are reported to Vancouver Coast Guard Radio on VHF Radio Channel 16. Be ready with a description of your vessel (name, type of vessel, size, colour), your location, and the nature of the accident. The Coast Guard can coordinate emergency and rescue operations. A Marine Radio Operator's Certificate is required to operate a VHF radio. The certificate is obtained through the Ministry of Communications, Lower Mainland District Office, 800 Burrard Street, Vancouver, telephone (604) 666-5468, or the Surrey Office, 3884–192nd Street, Surrey, telephone (604) 576-8691. Please note that Coast Guard officials allow unlicensed operators to call for help in an emergency.

DIVE STORES   Dive stores offer retail sales, instruction, equipment servicing, rentals, air, activities, trips, and charters. The Greater Vancouver area has sixteen dive stores, and Squamish has one. These stores are listed below. Consult the Yellow Pages or the White Pages for updated store locations and phone numbers.

AB Diver's World
1817 West 4th Avenue
Vancouver, BC V6J 1M4
(604) 732-1344

Adrenalin Sports
1512 Duranleau Street
Vancouver, BC V6H 3S4
(604) 682-2881

15

Capilano Diver's Supply
1236 Marine Drive
North Vancouver, BC V7P 1T3
(604) 986-0302

Cross Current Divers
14–2773 Barnett Highway
Coquitlam, BC V3B 1C2
(604) 944-2780

Deep Cove Dive Shop
4342 Gallant Avenue
North Vancouver, BC V6G 1K8
(604) 929-3116

The Diving Locker
2745 West 4th Avenue
Vancouver, BC V6K 1P9
(604) 736-2681

Dive and Sea Sports
825 McBride Boulevard
New Westminster, BC V3L 5B5
(604) 524-1188

Divers West
1709 West 4th Avenue
Vancouver, BC V6J 1M3
(604) 737-2822

Get Wet Adventures (The Outdoor Store)
20305 Fraser Highway
Langley, BC V3A 4E8

G and S Scuba and Sport
2210 2nd Avenue
Squamish, BC V0N 3G0
(604) 898-1575

The Great Pacific Diving Company
167–10020 152nd Street
Surrey, BC V3R 8X8
(604) 583-1700

Odyssey Diving Centre
2659 Kingsway
Vancouver, BC V5R 5H4
(604) 430-1451

Ocean Pro Divers
2–3189 King George Highway
Surrey, BC V4P 1B8
(604) 538-5608

Rowand's Reef
125–6080 Airport Road S
Richmond, BC V7B 1B4
(604) 273-0704

UBC Aqua Society
6138 Student Union Boulevard, UBC
Vancouver, BC V6T 2A5
(604) 228-3329

West Coast Scuba Centre
20–2755 Lougheed Highway
Port Coquitlam, BC V3B 5Y9
(604) 942-4838

The Wet Shop Diving and Water Sports
Centre
6371 Bruce Street
Horseshoe Bay, BC V7W 2G5
(604) 921-6371

DIVE CLUBS The following dive clubs in the Greater Vancouver area offer trips, activities, newsletters, and a chance to meet new dive buddies.

The Coquitlam Scuba Club meets the first Wednesday of each month at 7:30 p.m. at the Coquitlam Social Recreation Centre, 630 Poirier Street, Coquitlam.

The Fraser Valley Aquanutts meet the first Wednesday of each month at 7:00 p.m. at Mouat School in Clearbrook during the winter months. Summer meeting places vary. They can be contacted by writing to the Fraser Valley Aquanutts, c/o P.O. Box 281, Abbotsford, BC, V2S 4N9.

Off the Wall Dive and Social Club meets the second Friday of each month at 7:30 p.m. in Room 2804 of Douglas College, 700 Royal Avenue, New Westminster.

The Pescaderos meet the last Tuesday of each month at 7:30 p.m. at the False Creek Yacht Club, 1661 Granville Street, Vancouver.

The Richmond Aqua Addicts meet the second Thursday of each month at 8:00 p.m., in Committee Room A of the Brighouse Pavilion, on the southeast corner of Granville and Minoru in Richmond.

The Pacific Northwest Scuba Challenge Association (PNWSCA) offers instruction and diving opportunities to people with physical disabilities and is open to able-bodied and disabled, divers and non-divers. The club meets the third Thursday of each month at 7:30 p.m. in the boardroom of G. F. Strong Rehabilitation Centre, 4255 Laurel Avenue, Vancouver.

The Underwater Archaeological Society of British Columbia (UASBC) is dedicated to the exploration and preservation of the province's marine heritage. Meetings are held the last Wednesday of each month at 7:30 p.m. in the Finning Gallery of the Maritime Museum, 1905 Ogden Avenue, Vancouver.

The Marine Life Sanctuary Society of British Columbia is dedicated to the preservation of representative areas of the B.C. marine environment in their natural state. The aim of the group is to establish underwater parks where taking or harvesting of marine life of any kind is forbidden. For more information, contact the Marine Life Sanctuary Society, P.O. Box 48299, Bentall Centre, Vancouver, BC, V7X 1A1, (604) 929-4131.

DIVE CHARTERS   Dive charter vessels come in all shapes and sizes. Divers seeking only basic transportation to known sites can use vessels of opportunity such as water taxis. Boat charter companies offer both bare boat charters, for experienced boaters, and skippered charters. An intriguing recent addition to the list of vessels for hire is the diving kayak; check with kayaking companies for details on size, capacity, and availability.

Dedicated dive boats are harder to find. One such vessel is the *Adventure IV*, run by Seagoing Adventures, 231 Moray Street, Port Moody, BC, V3H 3T5; telephone (604) 461-3186. Some local dive stores periodically arrange dive charters to sites in Howe Sound and Indian Arm. Check to see if any trips are heading out from your favourite store.

Dive chartering is a specialized field. Not all charter companies can adequately provide for the special needs of divers. Divers seeking to charter a boat should enquire into the boat's fitness and layout to ensure that the boat is suitable for divers. Sufficient medical and emergency equipment to deal with accidents involving the use of compressed air should be on board. The crew should be trained and certified in boat handling and dive supervision, should know the site where the dives will be conducted, and should take into account the experience and training of the charter group before starting the dive.

MARINE LIFE IDENTIFICATION   The Vancouver Aquarium has displays of local marine life with information plaques on each display. The aquarium gift shop sells marine life identification and fact books and a video, *Ocean Under Glass in Stanley Park*.

Andy Lamb's Marine Identification Course is an excellent way for divers to improve their knowledge of marine life. Lamb is a local marine biologist and author. For more information, write to Andy Lamb, 3171 Huntleigh Crescent, North Vancouver, BC, V7H 1C9, (604) 929-4131.

Recommended publications:

Exploring the Seashore: A Guide to Shorebirds and Intertidal Plants and Animals, by Gloria Snively. Published by Gordon Soules Book Publishers.

Tidepool and Reef, by Rick Harbo. Published by Hancock House.

Guide to Western Seashore, by Rick Harbo. Published by Hancock House.

Edible Seashore, by Rick Harbo. Published by Hancock House.

Coastal Fishes of the Pacific Northwest, by Andy Lamb and Phil Edghill. Published by Harbour Publishing.

The Audubon Society Field Guide series, published by Alfred A. Knopf, including the following:
Field Guide to North American Seashore Creatures
Field Guide to Seashells
Field Guide to Fishes, Whales and Dolphins

The Audubon Society Nature Guide Pacific Coast, by Baydarth and Evelyn McConnaughey. Published in Canada by Random House.

Pacific Fishes of Canada, by J. L. Hart. Published as Bulletin 180 by the Department of Fisheries and Oceans.

Seashore Life of the Northern Pacific Coast, by Eugene Kozloff. Published by Douglas and McIntyre.

Pacific Coast Nudibranchs, by David W. Behrens. Published by University of Washington Press.

Beneath Puget Sound, by Peter Ward. Published by Peanut Butter Publishing.

Keys to the Marine Invertebrates of Puget Sound, the San Juan Archipelago and Adjacent Regions, by Eugene Kozloff. Published by University of Washington Press.

Seashore Life of Puget Sound, the Strait of Georgia and the San Juan Archipelago, by Eugene Kozloff. Published by J. J. Douglas.

Living Shores of the Pacific Northwest, by Lynwood Smith. Published by Pacific Search.

Pacific Coast Subtidal Invertebrates, by Dan Gotshall and Laurence Laurent. Published by Sea Challengers.

Field Book of Pacific Northwest Sea Creatures, by Dan McLachlan and Jak Ayres. Published by Naturegraph.

A Guide to Our Underwater World, by Joe Liburdi and Harry Truitt. Published by Superior Publishing/Hancock House.

Between Pacific Tides (5th edition), by Edward Ricketts and Jack Calvin. Published by Stanford University Press.

A Guide to Marine Coastal Plankton and Marine Invertebrate Larvae, by Deboyd Smith. Published by Kendall Hund Publishing Company.

Treasures of the Sea—Marine Life of the Pacific Northwest, by James Cribb. Published by Oxford University Press.

Seashore Animals of the Pacific Coast, by Myrtle Johnson and Harry Snook. Published by Dover Publications.

Pacific Marine Life—A Survey of Pacific Ocean Invertebrates, by Charles and Diana DeLuca. Published by Charles E. Tuttle.

Pacific Seashore—A Guide to Intertidal Ecology, by Thomas Carefoot. Published by Douglas and McIntyre.

Marine Wildlife of Puget Sound, the San Juans and the Strait of Georgia, by Steve Yates. Published by Globe Pequot Press.

Beach Walker—Sea Life of the West Coast, by Stephani Hewlett-Paine. Published by Douglas and McIntyre.

The Intertidal Bivalves of British Columbia, by D. B. Quayle. Provincial Museum Handbook #17.

Guide to the Marine Life of British Columbia, by Clifford Carl. Provincial Museum Handbook #21.

The Seastars of British Columbia, by Philip Lambert. Provincial Museum Handbook #39.

The Department of Fisheries and Oceans publishes fact sheets and pamphlets that are informative, easy to read, and well illustrated. They cover fisheries resources and phenomena and have reference lists for further reading. Subjects of interest to B.C. divers include cetaceans of Canada, dungeness crab, harbour seal, lingcod, marine fish eggs and larvae, northern shrimp, oyster, Pacific herring, Pacific salmon, red tides, redfish (ocean perch), rockfish, sea cucumber, sea scallop, selected shrimps of British Columbia, spiny dogfish, squid, and thorny and smooth skates. The fact sheets and pamphlets and a list of other titles and information are available from

Director of Communications
Department of Fisheries and Oceans
Suite 412
555 West Hastings Street
Vancouver, BC V6B 5G3
(604) 666-3169

Also available through the Department of Fisheries and Oceans is an Environment Canada pamphlet, *British Columbia Guide to Safe Mollusc Harvesting*.

Marine life slates are made of laminated plastic and can thus get wet without disintegrating.

Mac's Field Guide to Northwest Coastal Invertebrates

Mac's Field Guide to Northwest Coastal Fish

CHARTS AND OTHER MARINE PUBLICATIONS The Hydrographic Services Office provides a series of nautical charts helpful to divers trying to find their way on and under the surface of the water. Most are available from marine supply stores. *The Catalogue of Nautical Charts and Related Publications* is available free from the Institute of Ocean Sciences, Patricia Bay, P.O. Box 6000, Sidney, BC, V8L 4B2 and from local marine stores.

The following charts deal with the Vancouver area:

Chart 3311—Sunshine Coast, Vancouver Harbour to Desolation Sound. Strip chart coverage from the tip of Indian Arm west including all of Howe Sound.

Chart 3495—Vancouver Harbour, Eastern Portion. Indian Arm from the mouth of Indian River to Roche Point, including Port Moody.

Chart 3494—Vancouver Harbour, Central Portion. Admiralty Point west to Neptune Bank with Second Narrows inset.

Chart 3493—Vancouver Harbour, Western Portion. The Inner Harbour and False Creek area.

Chart 3481—Approaches to Vancouver Harbour. English Bay to the Second Narrows Bridge, including southeastern Howe Sound.

Chart 3526—Howe Sound. All of Howe Sound from the mouth of the Squamish River south to Gibsons and east to First Narrows.

Chart 3534—Plans—Howe Sound. Channels and harbours in Howe Sound, including Mannion Bay, Snug Cove, Fishermans Cove, Horseshoe Bay, Shoal Channel, and Squamish Harbour.

Chart L/C 3463—Strait of Georgia, Southern Portion. The southern Strait with the southeast corner of Howe Sound included.

Chart L/C 3512—Strait of Georgia, Central Portion. The central Strait including Howe Sound to a few kilometres (nautical miles) from the mouth of the Squamish River.

Notices to Mariners is a weekly publication that gives important marine information and corrections to charts and related publications. It is available free of charge from
Director, Aids and Waterways
Canadian Coast Guard
Ministry of Transport
Ottawa, ON K1A 0N7

British Columbia Small Craft Guide, volume 2. Contains descriptions of the B.C. coastline including the Vancouver area. Check for the most recent edition.

Sailing Directions, British Columbia Coast, volume 1. Geared towards large vessels. Contains detailed descriptions of the coastline and other information useful to mariners.

List of Lights, Buoys and Fog Signals. Published annually. Describes the size, shape, and characteristics of lights, buoys, and signals along the coast and inland.

Contact the Canadian Hydrographic Service for information on local dealers and available charts and publications or to order charts and publications directly:

Chart Sales and Distribution Office
Canadian Hydrographic Service
Department of Fisheries and Oceans
Institute of Ocean Sciences, Patricia Bay
9860 West Saanich Road
Sidney, BC V8L 4B2
(604) 363-6358   Fax: (604) 363-6390

Other publications:

Canadian Tide and Current Tables are published annually by the Department of Fisheries and Oceans. Volume 5, *Juan de Fuca Strait and Strait of Georgia*, covers the Vancouver area. It is available at marine stores, fishing and tackle shops, and dive stores.

West Coast Marine Weather Hazards Manual, A Guide to Local Forecasts and Conditions. Published by Gordon Soules Book Publishers. Includes information on storms, wind, sea conditions, weather, and local hazards of the B.C. coast.

Oceanography of the British Columbia Coast, by Richard E. Thompson. Published by the Department of Fisheries and Oceans.

Cruising the Sunshine Coast, by Bill Wolferstan. Published by Whitecap Books.

Shipwrecks of British Columbia and *More Shipwrecks of British Columbia*, by Fred Rogers. Published by Douglas and McIntyre.

Fisheries and Oceans publishes *Sport Fishing Guide British Columbia Tidal Waters*, which outlines fisheries regulations for surface and spear fishing and collection of shellfish, shrimp, prawns, and crab. It is available at most marine stores and tackle shops.

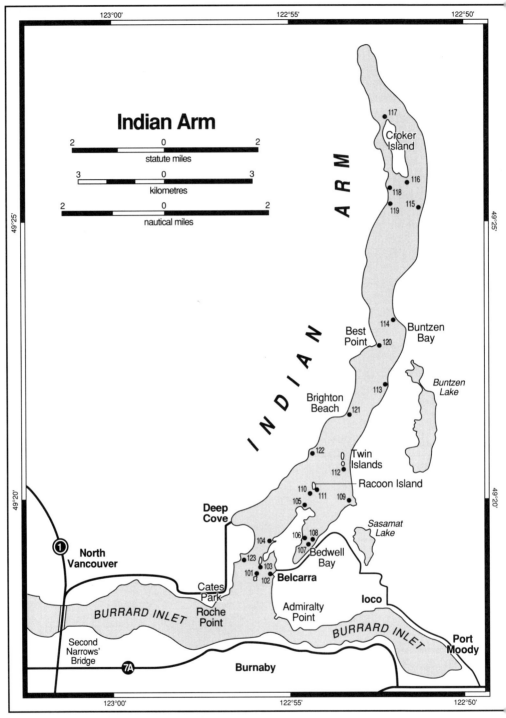

Indian Arm

statute miles

kilometres

nautical miles

123°00' 122°55' 122°50'

49°25'

49°20'

A R M

I N D I A N

Croker
Island

117

116
118
119 115

Buntzen
Bay

114
Best
Point 120

Buntzen
Lake

113

Brighton
Beach 121

122
Twin
Islands

112

Racoon Island

110
105 111 109

Deep
Cove

104 106 108
107 Bedwell
Bay

Sasamat
Lake

North
Vancouver 123 103
101
102 Belcarra

Cates
Park
Roche
Point

Admiralty
Point

Ioco

Port
Moody

Second
Narrows'
Bridge

BURRARD INLET

BURRARD INLET

Burnaby

101. Boulder Island
102. Belcarra Marker
103. Hamber Island Marker
104. Whiskey Cove
105. Jug Island
106. The Wreck of the
     Western Dispatcher

107. Wreck of the VT 100
     (previously thought to
     be HMS Cranbrook)
108. Bedwell Bay Reef
109. Belvedere Rock
110. Black Shoal
111. Racoon Island

112. Twin Islands
113. Buntzen Plant South
114. Buntzen Island
115. Boulder Bank
116. The Fishbowl/
     Croker Island South
117. Croker Island North

118. Rockfish Wall
119. Powell Bay
120. Best Point
121. Brighton Cliffs
122. Lone Rock Point
     (also called Woodlands)
123. Grey Rocks Island
     (also called Strathcona)

Part Two: Diving in Indian Arm

Indian Arm is a fjord 22 kilometres (12 nautical miles) long and 1.5 kilometres (.8 nautical mile) wide, northeast of downtown Vancouver. Its southern end runs along a line from Burns Point, near Port Moody, to Roche Point, on the North Vancouver side of Burrard Inlet. The northern boundary is marked by the mouth of the Indian River. Set in the rugged Coast Mountains, the Arm combines spectacular mountain scenery with a variety of dive sites. The underwater geography mirrors the above-water terrain. In the northern section, drop-offs, fissures, cracks, and overhangs provide crannies for life to inhabit and divers to explore. Depths can exceed 100 feet near shore, while those in mid-channel are more than 600 feet. Dives in the southern section of Indian Arm consist of gently sloping, boulder-strewn silt and sand bottoms. Fish, crabs, shrimp, plumose anemones, and sea stars flourish. Bottoms generally drop at a gentle or medium slope to maximum depths of 250 to 300 feet.

The central and northern sections of Indian Arm are accessible by boat only. Roadways end near Belcarra on the east side and Woodlands on the west. Dives in the south include both shore dives and boat dives.

The Vancouver Harbour Master's office requests that any groups conducting organized dives in Indian Arm contact the office at 666-2405 during business hours or 666-6011 weekends and evenings to inform them of the activity.

Facilities in Indian Arm are limited. Washrooms, telephones, and temporary docking facilities are available at Belcarra Park and Cates Park. Public docks are also available at Deep Cove and Twin Islands. Fuel docks at Deep Cove Marina and Reed Point Marina provide fuel, oil, fishing gear, marine supplies, and a limited supply of food. There are boat launch ramps at Cates Park, Deep Cove, Reed Point, and Rocky Point.

101. Boulder Island

Boat dive...shallow site with gently sloped sand bottom strewn with rocks and boulders...colourful site, especially towards west side...rocks covered in plumose anemone colonies...shrimp and sea stars common...hazards are boat traffic, current, and red jellyfish

Skill level   1 or 2 (see page 11)

Access   Boat dive

Location   Boulder Island is .7 kilometre (.4 nautical mile) west of Belcarra Park in southern Indian Arm. The dive site is along the northern tip and west side of the island. Anchorage is available in the shallow water around the north tip of the island in good holding ground. Because of the shallow rocks near the island, care should be exercised when anchoring. Descend the anchor line and explore.

Hazards   Boat traffic, current, and red jellyfish (see page 12)

Description   Boulder Island is a shallow, colourful dive close to the city and the facilities of Belcarra Park. The site is easy to find and to dive. A sand bottom slopes gently away from the island. Large boulders and rocks scattered on the bottom provide habitat for many sea creatures. The boulders are at their thickest and largest near the shore. Depths run from 15 to 50 feet. Most of the life is concentrated between 20 and 30 feet.

The west side of the island is a colourful and interesting place. Bunches of orange and white plumose anemones stand like beacons on the rocks. The bottom is thick with darting coonstripe shrimp. Sunflower stars, leather stars, and short-spined stars prowl the rocks and the sand. California cucumbers, white cucumbers, and orange cucumbers lie in wait around the rocks. Flabellina salmonacea nudibranchs huddle in bunches on top of boulders. Buried and painted tealia anemones, light bulb tunicates, ostrich plume hydroids, and false Pacific jingle shells are also common.

Around the north tip of Boulder Island, divers find blue top snails, hermit crabs, and decorator crabs. Dungeness and red rock crabs scurry along the bottom. Bottles thick with barnacles lie everywhere. Schooling fish such as striped perch, shiner perch, and tube snouts wander through the water. Lingcod and rockfish prefer to stick close to the bottom or hide in large crevices in the rock.

The west side of the island seen from the south

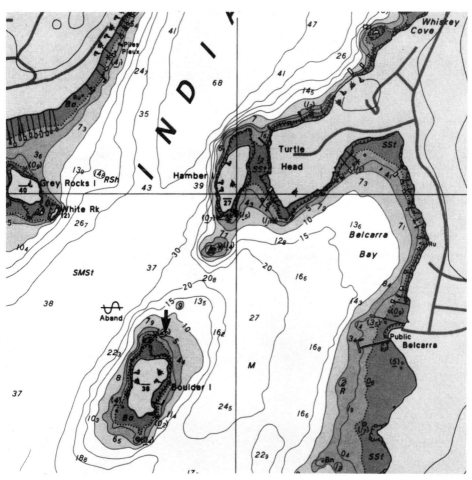

NOT TO BE USED FOR NAVIGATION—see page 9.
Use Canadian chart 3495 for navigation.
For information on obtaining navigational charts, see page 21.

25

102. Belcarra Marker

Shore dive. . .shallow rocky outcropping offshore. . .depth to 35 feet. . .simple shallow dive with good variety of fish and sea stars. . .swim out has some attractions, particularly hooded nudibranchs. . .hazards are current and boat traffic

Skill level   1 or 2 (see page 11)

Access   Shore dive

Location   Belcarra Marker is in the southern section of Belcarra Park in southeastern Indian Arm. From the Barnet Highway, take the loco Road turnoff and follow the signs to loco Road. Follow loco to First Avenue and turn right. First Avenue becomes Bedwell Bay Road. Stay on Bedwell Bay Road until the signs for Belcarra Park lead you to the parking lot. On the right is the dock; on the left, perched on a cement base approximately 150 metres offshore, is a white circular tower. Snorkel to the marker and descend, or take a compass bearing and fin along the bottom.

Hazards   Current and boat traffic (see page 12)

Description   Belcarra Marker warns boaters of a group of offshore rocks that are close to the surface at low tide. The rocks and shallow waters surrounding them make an ideal little dive spot for those looking for a quick splash near picnic and park facilities. The base of the rocks meets a flat sand bottom in 25 to 35 feet of water. Closer to shore, the bottom turns to mud with forests of eelgrass.

Hooded nudibranchs, some very large, live on the eelgrass. Dungeness and red rock crabs, leather stars, sunflower stars, and clams live in the mud. Out on the rocks, barnacles cluster in large groups and wave fans through the water, filtering for food. Shrimp are everywhere, hiding in cracks or standing out in the open. Kelp leaves and purple stars cover the upper rocks. Sunflower and short-spined stars prowl the lower levels. Small rock crabs and hermit crabs scuttle up and down. White, grey, and orange plumose anemones add colour, as do orange cucumbers, ochre stars, and painted brittle stars. Chitons and limpets are glued in place. Schools of shiner perch, pile perch, and tube snouts swim through the water. Kelp greenlings, sailfin sculpins, and lingcod are also found.

Wheelchair access   Either enter at the dock for easy access and a long swim or manoeuvre down the path to the shore for a shorter swim.

The marker seen from the beach

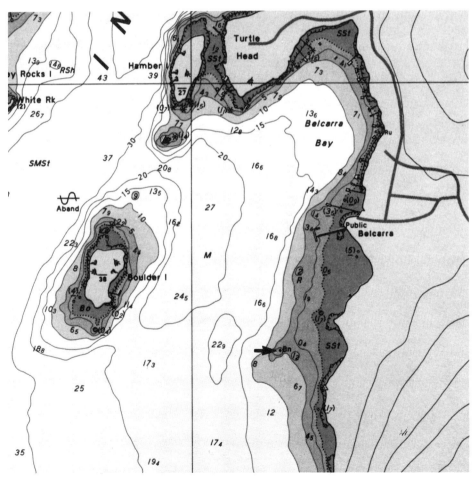

NOT TO BE USED FOR NAVIGATION—see page 9.
Use Canadian chart 3495 for navigation.
For information on obtaining navigational charts, see page 21.

27

103. Hamber Island Marker

Boat dive. . .depths to 90 or more. . .very good marine life mix, including big lingcod and little decorator crabs covered in live barnacles. . .hazards are current, boat traffic, and poor visibility

Skill level   3 (see page 11)

Access   Boat dive

Location   Hamber Island Marker is on the south end of Hamber Island, next to Belcarra Park in southern Indian Arm. It is a white circular tower with a red top band on a cement base. Anchorage is available to the southeast of the marker. The irregular rock to the west can make anchoring difficult and has even claimed the odd anchor.

Hazards   Current, boat traffic, and poor visibility (see page 12)

Description   Hamber Island is close to marina and launch facilities and yet provides a very interesting dive. One of the main reasons life is plentiful here is the current that washes over the reef. The rocky reef under Hamber Island Marker draws marine life to its deeper sections like a magnet. The west side is a steep drop with intermittent wall face, jagged rock, and deep cracks and crevices. Depths run to more than 90 feet. South of the marker is a medium slope with tumbled boulders and depths to 70 feet. On the east, a gentle sand slope littered with rocks provides the shallowest area of the site, reaching depths of no more than 40 to 50 feet.

Most of the life at this site congregates between 50 and 80 feet. Three or four large beds of white plumose anemones spring majestically out of the reef's west side. Ostrich plume hydroids, orange cucumbers, slippered cucumbers, and light bulb tunicates also stretch out into the water. Orange sunflower stars, ochre stars, blood stars, and California cucumbers prowl the rocky depths. Walls of acorn barnacles wave frantically for food. Small patches of these barnacles, adhered to decorator crabs, make a strange sight as they eat on the run. Giant barnacles, some overgrown by orange encrusting sponge, use large purple tentacles to trap their food. Also on the wall are false Pacific jingle shells stuck in place, alabaster nudibranchs and sea lemons crawling slowly, and hermit crabs running and tumbling. Shrimp are everywhere, darting about or hiding in crevices. A bit deeper in these crevices are hairy lithode crabs and copper and quillback rockfish. One of the most exciting moments of a dive here is a chance encounter with huge lingcod. Their size and permanent scowls stop you in your tracks. A little less intimidating are the schools of shiner perch and striped perch.

The shallow waters on the east side of the site are home to short-spined stars, leather stars, dungeness crabs, and some broad leafy kelp. Lined chitons grow on the scattered rocks.

The marker seen from the south

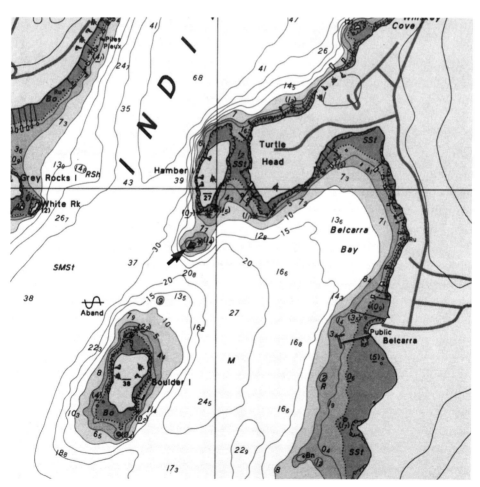

NOT TO BE USED FOR NAVIGATION—see page 9.
Use Canadian chart 3495 for navigation.
For information on obtaining navigational charts, see page 21.

29

104. Whiskey Cove

Shore dive. . .easy entry, short snorkel. . .rock wall with lots of small life. . .second wall just beyond first. . .depths to 70 feet. . .hazards are boat traffic and red jellyfish

Skill level   1 or 2 (see page 11)

Access   Shore dive

Location   Whiskey Cove is .8 kilometre north of Belcarra Park in southern Indian Arm. Follow directions to Belcarra Park and then continue on Bedwell Bay Road past the park until you come to a T-junction. Turn right onto Belcarra Bay Road and follow it until it intersects with Whiskey Cove Lane. At the southwest corner of the intersection is a small dirt parking lot with space for 8 to 10 cars. Park here and follow a short trail through the woods to a narrow bay. Snorkel out past the floats and docks to a large rock on the southwest side of the bay, descend, and move west.

Hazards   Boat traffic and red jellyfish (see page 12)

Description   With an easy entry, a controlled environment, and abundant small and medium-sized marine life, Whiskey Cove is a perfect patch dive. Divers can explore the flat rock face inch by inch in the calm water. Some ledges with scattered rocks and a second rock face past a narrow sand wedge can also be reached south of the main rock. Depths at the base of the rocks run from 25 to 70 feet.

Whiskey Cove is a dive site to explore slowly and carefully. Little gems adhere to the rock face. Beautiful janolus fuscus, cuthona, opalescent, alabaster, and brown spotted nudibranchs are everywhere. Tiny juvenile rock crabs with white striped carapaces, small multi-coloured hermit crabs, and other crab species are present in large numbers. Tidepool sculpins, scaleyhead sculpins, sole, flounder, coonstripe shrimp, and decorator crabs play along the rock face. Some large dungeness and red rock crabs also scuttle about. Sunflower stars, ochre stars, false Pacific jingle shells, mussels, and plumose anemones are found. Just off the wall, moon jellies, red jellyfish, schools of tube snouts, and striped perch hover in the water. In the sand at the base of the rock live pink short-spined stars and hundreds of buried dungeness and red rock crab.

Whiskey Cove is closed to divers between sunset and 8:00 a.m. Special use permits for these times can be obtained by phoning the Greater Vancouver Regional District (GVRD) at (604)432-6352.

Wheelchair access   The short dirt path to the shore should be negotiated with care. The site has a good entry/exit point.

Looking from the beach, past the private docks at the east side of the large rock

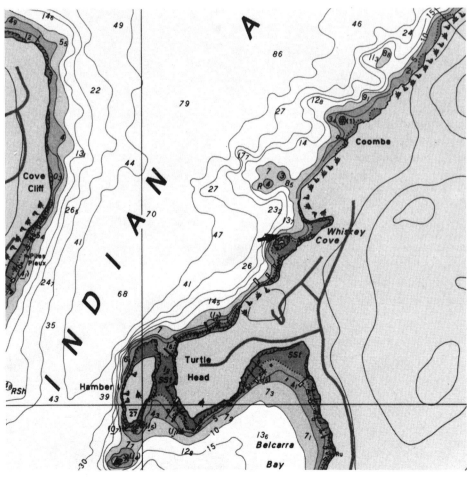

NOT TO BE USED FOR NAVIGATION—see page 9.
Use Canadian chart 3495 for navigation.
For information on obtaining navigational charts, see page 21.

31

105. Jug Island

Boat dive...short distance from launches...medium-sloped sand with odd rock wall...good variety of life including fish and nudibranchs...hazards are boat traffic and red jellyfish

Skill level   1 or 2 (see page 11)

Access   Boat dive

Location   Jug Island is 2 kilometres (1.1 nautical miles) north of Belcarra Park in south central Indian Arm. The dive site is the southwestern side of the island. Anchorage is available near the southwest tip of the island in 30 to 40 feet of water in fair holding ground. The bottom comes up quickly and forces boaters to anchor close to the island. Enter the water, descend, and move along the south side of the island.

Hazards   Boat traffic and red jellyfish (see page 12)

Description   Jug Island is a short boat ride away from the marinas and launch ramps of Indian Arm and well worth the trip. It is a good dive for beginners developing skills and experienced divers looking for a quick dive in the Arm. The bottom, of sand, silt, and crushed shell, has a medium slope with occasional steep slopes and small walls. Depths run to 60 feet or a bit deeper if experience and training allow. Rocks in the sand and crevices in the walls lie waiting to be explored.

The south side of Jug Island can be toured on one tank in a relaxed, easy dive. Divers can play with the thousands of shrimp hopping about the bottom. Slippered cucumbers and broad base sea squirts add some red colour to the rocks. Sunflower stars, leather stars, pink short-spined stars, and ochre stars move slowly throughout the site. Hiding in crevices are hairy lithode crabs, copper rockfish, and quillback rockfish. Some of the rockfish venture out in the open for a look at the scenery. Lingcod lie brooding on the rocks, fleeing when divers get too close. Blackeye gobies retreat into the safety of their homes dug out under the rocks. Schools of striped and shiner perch hover over the area. You may see the outline of a red rock or dungeness crab lying in wait with only its eyes poking out of the sand. Also in the sand are dendronotus diversicolor nudibranchs sporting orange-tipped cerata. Yellow margin and white nudibranchs live on the rocks and walls. White and orange plumose anemones are scattered about the site.

The southwest side of the island

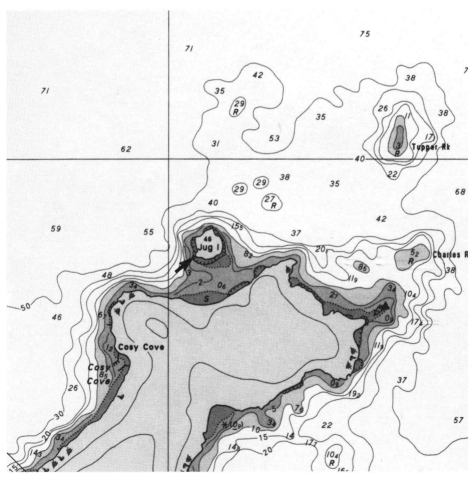

NOT TO BE USED FOR NAVIGATION—see page 9.
Use Canadian chart 3495 for navigation.
For information on obtaining navigational charts, see page 21.

33

106. The Wreck of the *Western Dispatcher*

Boat dive. . .wreck almost see-through, as most of the hull has been eaten away. . .some equipment and wiring still inside, some marine life on wreck. . .to north is small schooner with some life. . .depths to 70 feet. . .hazards are the wreck, boat traffic, and poor visibility

Skill level   2 or 3 (see page 11)

Access   Boat dive

Location   The wreck of the *Western Dispatcher* is on the western side of Bedwell Bay in southeastern Indian Arm. From the marker at the northeastern end of Bedwell Bay, travel 300 metres south along the shoreline. On a tree near the water's edge is a white sign marked Cable. Just past the sign is a steel cable fixed to a metal ring on the shore. Gear up and follow the cable under water to the *Western Dispatcher* and a smaller wreck close by. The cable may be submerged at high tides but is only a few feet from the surface, so it should be easy to find.

Hazards   The wreck, boat traffic, and poor visibility (see page 12)

Description   The *Western Dispatcher*, a former U.S. Navy vessel converted to a fish packer, is the larger of two wrecks lying on the bottom in northwest Bedwell Bay. An eerie wreck in the process of collapsing, the *Dispatcher* is unsafe to penetrate or even touch. It lies on an east/west line on its starboard side on the muddy bottom, with the keel in 65 to 75 feet of water. The second wreck, possibly a former sealing schooner, lies overturned in the mud about 30 meters north of the bow of the *Dispatcher* in 40 to 45 feet of water.

The *Western Dispatcher* is a spooky skeleton of a ship in a world where ships do not belong. Most of the wooden hull has been eaten away, leaving inner compartments, including a wire-strewn engine room, visible from the outside. The starboard side and the bow have begun to collapse, and, with so much of the rest of the hull missing, the entire vessel will suffer the same fate in the future. The upper house hangs at a rakish angle and is also collapsing upon itself. Much of the wiring, pipes, hoses, and storage tanks remain scattered throughout the wreck and plainly visible as you tour the outside. The steering gear remains in the stern section just behind the small cargo holds.

The transom of the *Dispatcher* is intact and still retains some green paint and the Roman numeral VII etched into it, but it is becoming overgrown with barnacles. The rudder is pinned in the mud under the vessel. On the starboard side is a debris field littered with various pieces of the wreck. Some marine life has taken up residence on the remains of the *Dispatcher*. Sunflower stars, ochre stars, alabaster nudibranchs, calcareous tube worms, shrimp, decorator and galathaeid crabs, and rockfish all live on or around the wreck.

The small schooner north of the *Western Dispatcher* also attracts marine life. Schools of tube snouts, shiner perch, striped perch, and rockfish hide in the overturned wreck or swim close to its hull. Plumose anemones spring from the keel. Coonstripe shrimp dart over, under, and through the wooden remains. Some interesting machinery lies scattered in the mud around the wreck.

The Cable sign that leads to the wrecks

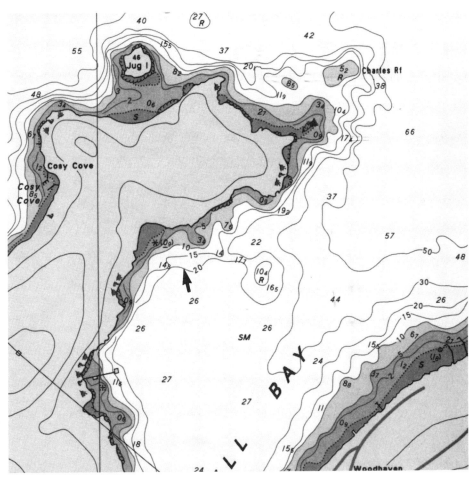

NOT TO BE USED FOR NAVIGATION—see page 9.
Use Canadian chart 3495 for navigation.
For information on obtaining navigational charts, see page 21.

35

107. **Wreck of the *VT 100*** (previously thought to be *HMS Cranbrook*)

Shore dive. . .wreck, with most of hull, bulkheads and decking gone. . .wiring, steering gear, some fittings remain. . .good variety of marine life. . .hazards are the wreck, boat traffic, and poor visibility

Skill level   2 (see page 11)

Access   Shore dive

Location   The *VT 100* lies in Bedwell Bay near Belcarra Park in southeastern Indian Arm. From Highway 7A take the loco Road turnoff and follow the signs to loco Road. Follow loco for 3.5 kilometres and turn right onto First Avenue. Drive along First, which turns into Bedwell Bay Road. Follow Bedwell Bay Road for 2.5 kilometres, and then turn left onto Main Avenue, right onto Kelly Road, and left onto Marine Avenue. Park on the gravel shoulder of Marine, 150 metres past its intersection with Kelly. A short sand and rock path leads to the beach. Immediately south of the beach is a large dock. The entry itself is marked by a large white boulder that is partly covered at high tide (see photo). From this boulder, follow a compass bearing of 330 degrees to a depth of 50 feet or else swim straight out to the 50 foot depth contour and then swim north at that depth for about 100 meters.

Hazards   The wreck, boat traffic, and poor visibility (see page 12)

Description   The *VT 100* combines the thrill of a recognizable wreck with the splendour of abundant marine life. The former U.S. Navy minesweeper *YMS 159* was being converted to a wood chip barge and renamed *Vancouver Tug and Barge #100* when it was set on fire and sunk by vandals in 1953. It lies on the muddy bottom slightly on its port side in 50 to 60 feet at the keel.

Most of the *VT 100* has been eaten away by shipworms, but the bulkheads still rise slab-like out of the lower deck. Hull and decking are still evident in the extreme bow and stern sections. The years of submersion have made these sections unsafe to enter or touch. Divers should only observe when diving the *VT 100*. Steering gear, rudders, pipes, wires, tanks, and fittings are left in the stern. The bow rises to 35 feet of water and still has some decking and compartments. A thick layer of silt coats the lower decks between bulkheads and can rise up, reducing visibility, if stirred by careless fins.

A large variety of marine life has taken up residence on the *VT 100*. Schools of shiner perch and striped perch dart playfully around the wreck. Quillback rockfish, copper rockfish, and lingcod drift lazily up and down, peering quizzically at divers. Coonstripe shrimp gather in abundance and dance away from divers. In the summer months, colourful opalescent nudibranchs swarm the wreck and lay ringlets of white eggs on any available flat surface. The bow and stern decking are covered with colonies of orange and white plumose anemones. Sea lemons, white and brown spotted nudibranchs, and rough mantle dorises also appear throughout. Various starfish, including sunflower stars, leather stars, blood stars, and short-spined stars, inhabit the wreck. Whelks, transparent tunicates, decorator and red rock crabs, encrusting sponges, ice cream cone worms, curly terebellid worms, and calcareous tube worms also live on the remains of the *VT 100*.

Wheelchair access   The dirt path to the beach must be negotiated with care. Once on the beach, disabled divers find this a great site.

The path leading to the water and the white rock from which a course of 330 degrees leads to the wreck

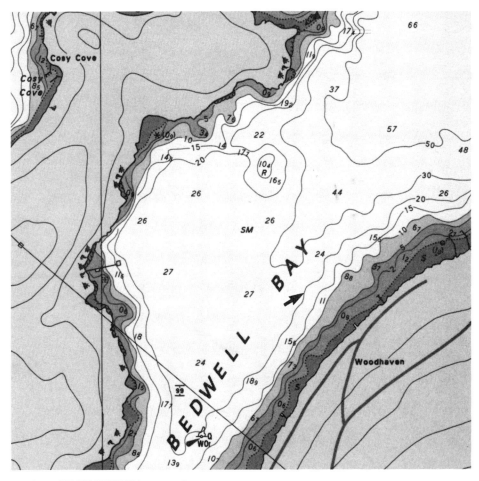

NOT TO BE USED FOR NAVIGATION—see page 9.
Use Canadian chart 3495 for navigation.
For information on obtaining navigational charts, see page 21.

37

108. Bedwell Bay Reef

Shore dive. . .rock dump "reef". . .gentle to medium slope to 65 feet. . .life on descent line as well as on reef and on an old cable at south end of reef. . .hazards are boat traffic and poor visibility

Skill level   1 (see page 11)

Access   Shore dive

Location   Bedwell Bay Reef is on the east side of Bedwell Bay in southern Indian Arm. From Highway 7A in Port Moody, take the loco Road exit and follow the signs to loco Road. Follow loco for 3.5 kilometres. Turn right onto First Avenue and follow it until it becomes Bedwell Bay Road. Drive along Bedwell Bay Road for 2.5 kilometres and then turn left onto Main Avenue. Turn right onto Kelly Road and then left onto Marine Avenue. Follow Marine for 150 metres and park on the sand and gravel shoulder. A short path leads to the beach. Once on the beach, divers should wade, walk, or snorkel, depending on the height of the tide, north towards the dock and boathouse complex. A short snorkel past the end of the dock leads to an orange mooring buoy. Descend the line attached to the buoy.

Hazards   Boat traffic and poor visibility (see page 12)

Description   The Bedwell Bay Reef has a good sampling of life and is an easy site to find and dive. Its proximity to the wreck of the *VT 100* makes it a natural choice as a second dive. The marine life begins as soon as you leave the surface. The mooring buoy and line sprout purple feather duster worms, skeleton shrimp, mussels, and various plants. The reef, a dumping ground of rocks and boulders, is approximately 30 feet wide and runs north/south at a gentle to medium slope under water from 30 to 65 feet deep. The base of the mooring buoy lies in 45 feet of water.

Divers are greeted by hordes of coonstripe shrimp when they descend to the Bedwell Bay Reef. Orange and white plumose anemones are scattered throughout the reef attached to the rocks. Buried tealia anemones can be found in the sand on either side. Dungeness, red rock, and decorator crabs are visible out in the open, and dungeness and red rock are also partly buried in the sand. Various fish also inhabit the area. Quillback and copper rockfish swim above the rocks and hide in crevices. Sailfin sculpins and blackeye gobies hide in small crevices, while sand dabs and other flatfish lie quietly camouflaged on the bottom. Divers can see whelks, glassy tunicates, hermit crabs, and lined chitons on the tops and side of rocks. Sunflower stars prowl the reef.

An old cable lying on an east/west line intersects the reef in 35 feet of water. Following the cable back towards shore is an interesting way to view a variety of creatures.

Wheelchair access   The dirt path to the beach must be negotiated with care. Once on the beach, disabled divers find this a great site.

The dock and mooring buoy that lead to the reef

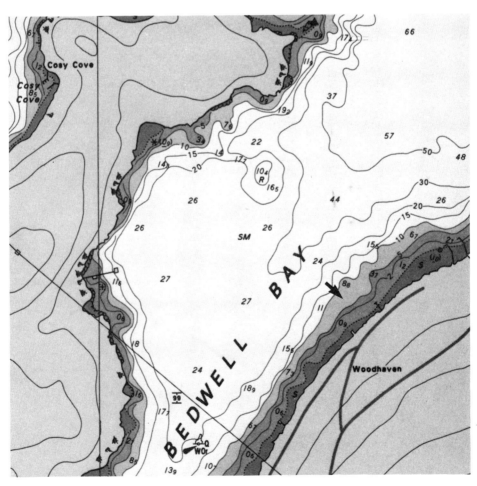

109. Belvedere Rock

Boat dive...depths from 10 to 85 feet...rocky pinnacle with boulders, small walls, and gentle slopes spread out over large area...good mix of life...hazards are boat traffic and red jellyfish

Skill level   1, 2, or 3 (see page 11)

Access   Boat dive

Location   Belvedere Rock is in the centre of Farrer Cove, 1.3 kilometres (.7 nautical miles) north of the mouth of Bedwell Bay in southeastern Indian Arm. The rock is marked by an orange road pylon tied to a tire and anchored to a metal beam. Should this homemade marker have disappeared, line up the large brown flat-faced house on a bearing of 120 degrees magnetic, roughly 142 degrees true, 400 metres from shore, and move along that bearing until your depth sounder reads 20 to 30 feet. Anchorage is available anywhere on the site. The top of the rock is awash on very low tides, so extreme caution must be exercised when approaching and departing the site.

Hazards   Boat traffic and red jellyfish (see page 12)

Description   Belvedere Rock is a silt-covered rocky pinnacle that rises from 85 feet to near the surface. It is spread out over a large area and includes gentle slopes, small walls, and boulders dotting the rocky bottom. Divers can explore shallow to moderate depths, depending on training and experience. The site is somewhat barren past 80 feet.

Belvedere Rock is ideal for those who like to cover a large area on a dive. A tour of the varied bottom rewards divers with a view of some colourful vegetation and a good collection of marine animals. Bright red surfgrass, red and green sea lettuce, and brown kelp grow in the shallow waters. Thousands of brown and neon blue shrimp, coonstripe shrimp, and prawns scurry over the bottom. The unlucky ones run into the tentacles of waiting orange and white plumose anemones. Dungeness and red rock crabs lie buried in the silt or dash away from approaching divers. Galathaeid crabs, eelpouts, and blackeye gobies live near rocks and boulders and duck into cracks and holes at the first sign of trouble. Decorator crabs perch on top of rocks and challenge with outstretched claws all who pass their way. Ochre stars, broad base squirts, tritons, flabellina salmonacea nudibranchs, orange nudibranchs, and white nudibranchs all live at various depths along the site. In the deepest sections, rows of small barnacles crowd the rocks. Hovering above the pinnacle are schools of tube snouts and lots of quillback rockfish.

The homemade marker float; beyond, the house that serves as an alternative reference

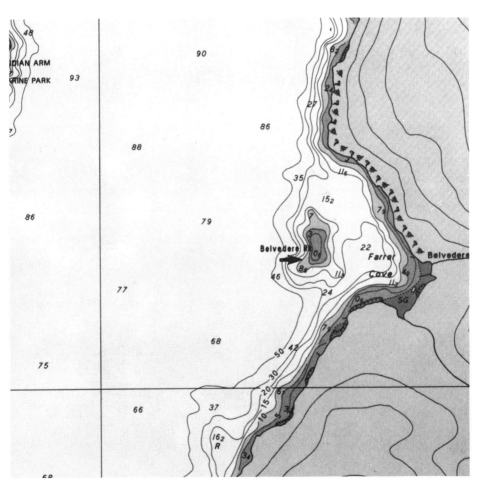

NOT TO BE USED FOR NAVIGATION—see page 9.
Use Canadian chart 3495 for navigation.
For information on obtaining navigational charts, see page 21.

41

110. Black Shoal

Boat dive. . .two rocky pinnacles on sand base at 40 to 80 feet rise to 15 feet from surface. . .very unusual marine life, especially the fish and shrimp. . .hazards are boat traffic and red jellyfish

Skill level   1 or 3 (see page 11)

Access   Boat dive

Location   Black Shoal is 200 metres southwest of Racoon Island in southern Indian Arm. The shoal has two pinnacles, which come to within 15 feet of the surface on very low tides. To locate them, anchor just off the southeast tip of Racoon Island, gear up, and descend. Once under water, move in a southerly direction and follow the sand bottom to the rocky base of the pinnacles.

Hazards   Boat traffic and red jellyfish (see page 12)

Description   It is hard to miss these two underwater hills just south of Racoon Island and harder still to miss the unusual marine life gathered here. Black Shoal is a site to test any marine identification skills. Bring your identification books and prepare to search after diving this spot. With depths varying from 15 to 80 feet and averaging 35, divers can spend quite a bit of time searching the area for new and interesting species of fish and invertebrates. Occasional boulders make the search all the more fun.

The most numerous inhabitants of Black Shoal are the shrimp. Coonstripe and clown shrimp are everywhere. Also at the site are brown shrimp with blue neon spots. The variety of fish in this area is remarkable. CO sole, sand dabs, starry flounders, mottled sole, brown rockfish, black kelp greenlings, buffalo sculpins, blackeye gobies, and copper rockfish can all be seen. Little hairy lithode crabs lie wedged in the rock. Hermit crabs, decorator crabs, red rock crabs, and a few dungeness appear in spots. Nudibranchs are represented by white, yellow margin, janolus fuscus, and sea lemon varieties. Orange and white plumose anemones stand sentry atop the rocks. Swimming anemones stretch orange and white striped tentacles into the water. Yellow boring sponge, lacy bryozoans, false Pacific jingle shells, and swimming scallops adhere to the pinnacle. Hovering in the waters above the bottom are sea gooseberries, moon jellies, red jellyfish, and sea butterflies.

Racoon Island Marine Park sign

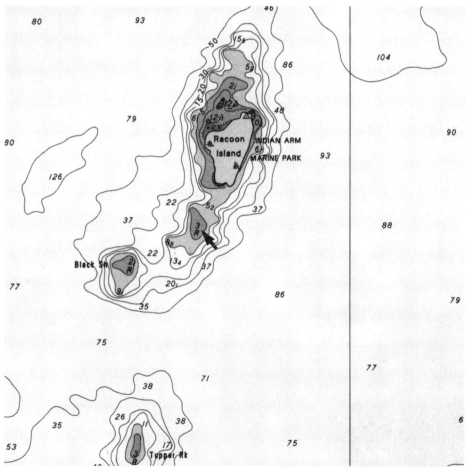

43

111. Racoon Island

Boat dive...medium-sloped bottom of rock and sand...depths to 100 feet or more...bottom is alive with shrimp...good mix of invertebrates spread out over a large area...main hazards are boat traffic, depth, and red jellyfish

Skill level   2 or 3 (see page 11)

Access   Boat dive

Location   Racoon Island is 1.5 kilometres (.8 nautical mile) northwest of Bedwell Bay in southern Indian Arm. The dive site is along the entire length of the eastern side of the island. Anchorage is available on the southeastern tip of the island in shallow water. Caution should be exercised when anchoring, as a shallow rocky reef that extends from the island is covered by all but the lowest tides. Enter at the southeast tip of the island and move north.

Hazards   Boat traffic, depth, and red jellyfish (see page 12)

Description   Racoon Island is a bright dive perfect for those who like to cover a lot of territory while under water. Shallow or deep, it holds many interesting sights. The medium to steep bottom drops to 100 feet or more. It alternates between sand/crushed shell bottom and craggy, sometimes jagged, rock formations. Most of the life lies in 80 feet or less, obligingly out in the open for easy sightings.

The southeastern tip of the island has a rocky reef and small rock wall covered in orange, grey, and purply blue sunflower stars. White plumose anemones also appear in the shallower spots. Move north, and deeper divers see decorator crabs, calcareous tube worms, orange and tan cup corals, and slippered cucumbers.

By this time, you may have noticed that the bottom seems to move. Focus on it and you will see thousands of colourful shrimp darting about the sand and rock. Look carefully into cracks and thousands more stare out. This is a wonderful sight during a night dive, as their eyes shine pink in the beam of an underwater light. Competing for space in the cracks are quillback rockfish, galathaeid crabs, and blackeye gobies. Out in the open are lacy bryozoans; broad based sea squirts; white, yellow margin, and brown spotted nudibranchs; orange plumose anemones; tube-dwelling anemones; ochre stars; Pacific pink scallops; and red rock crabs.

In the shallower sections, kelp, mussels, and barnacles grow profusely. Just off the bottom or hovering in mid-water are the odd lingcod, yelloweye rockfish, sea gooseberry, moon jelly, and red jellyfish.

The eastern side of the island seen from the south

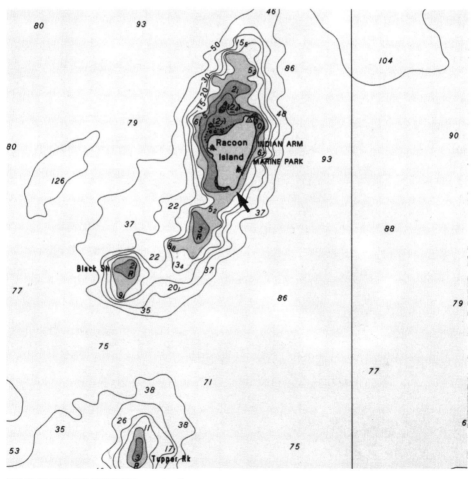

NOT TO BE USED FOR NAVIGATION—see page 9.
Use Canadian chart 3495 for navigation.
For information on obtaining navigational charts, see page 21.

45

112. Twin Islands

Boat dive. . .mixed sand/silt, boulder, rock bottom. . .some small ledges and walls. . .good variety of marine life. . .depths to 65 feet. . .hazards are boat traffic and red jellyfish

Skill level   1 (see page 11)

Access   Boat dive

Location   Twin Islands are 4.1 kilometres (2.2 nautical miles) north of Belcarra Park on the eastern side of central Indian Arm. The dive site is the southern tip of the south island. Anchorage is available directly south of the tip of the island in shallow water with good holding ground. A B.C. Marine Park sign at the south tip of the southern island can be used as an anchoring and site reference. When you enter the water, explore the south tip and along the east side of the island.

Hazards   Boat traffic and red jellyfish (see page 12)

Description   The south section of Twin Islands offers an easy descent to moderate depths along a compact yet varied bottom. The sand/shell bottom moves at a gentle slope to 30 to 40 feet and then down to 60 to 65 feet at a medium slope. Rocks and rocky outcroppings pop up in places, and there are some interesting rock formations, small walls, and ledges on the east side of the site. Boulders occupy much of the shallow water near the southern tip of the island. Divers can go deeper than 65 feet if they have the necessary training and experience, but the marine life thins out past this level.

Twin Islands' southern extremity is a relaxing site to tour. The varied bottom attracts vegetation such as eel grass, rockweed, sea lettuce, and kelp. It also provides habitat for a good mix of marine animals. Hooded nudibranchs, pink short-spined stars, moon jellies, and red rock crabs live around the eel grass. Plumose and painted tealia anemones cluster on rocks, while tube-dwelling anemones grow in the sand. Leather stars, purple stars, and blue and orange sunflower stars are found on the shallow boulders. Ochre stars are in deeper water. In the crevices and rock walls of the east side of the site are slippered cucumbers, orange cucumbers, broad base squirts, and curly terebellid worms. Chitons and false Pacific jingle shells glue themselves to rocks throughout the area. Dungeness crabs choose a sandy bottom as their home, while decorator and hermit crabs prefer the rocks. Long, thin California cucumbers, giant coonstripe shrimp, and glowing neon clown shrimp seem not to care and are found on any bottom type. Gobies, shiner perch, and striped perch are also seen at this site.

The Twin Islands Marine Park sign

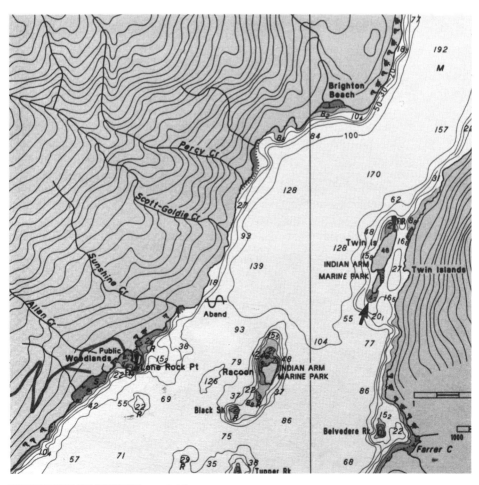

NOT TO BE USED FOR NAVIGATION—see page 9.
Use Canadian chart 3495 for navigation.
For information on obtaining navigational charts, see page 21.

47

113. Buntzen Plant South

Boat dive. . .medium-sloped sand bottom with boulders, walls, ledges, and a rock slide. . .life typically found in sand and in rocky areas. . .hazards are depth and red jellyfish

Skill level   2 or 3 (see page 11)

Access   Boat dive

Location   The Buntzen Power Plant is 4.6 kilometres (2.5 nautical miles) north of the mouth of Bedwell Bay in central Indian Arm. The plant consists of two buildings .75 kilometre apart on the eastern side of the Arm. The dive site is south of the southern building. Anchorage is available near the shore in shallow water, on a small ledge 200 metres south of the plant. Follow the anchor line down and move north.

Hazards   Depth and red jellyfish (see page 12)

Description   Buntzen Plant South is one of the few sloped sand bottoms in the steep, rocky world of central Indian Arm. The unusual sand bottom found in the area makes for easier anchorage and diving than at other sites in central Indian Arm. Medium-sloped sand, strewn with boulders, ledges, and occasional wall-like drops, descends past 100 feet. A thin silt coating is on the ledges. In the northern section of the site, rocks cascade downward along the sloped bottom.

   The mixture of sand and rocks of different shapes and sizes attracts marine life not seen in other parts of central Indian Arm. Tube-dwelling anemones, burrowing anemones, clams, short-spined stars, and red rock crabs live in the sand. The rocks and boulders have much of the same life as other sites in this area, with schooling striped perch, copper rockfish, quillback rockfish, blackeye gobies, and coonstripe shrimp gathering in large numbers. Also around the rocky sections of the dive are calcareous tube worms, slippered cucumbers, and broad base squirts. Barnacles lie covered in orange encrusting sponge. Orange, yellow, and white encrusting sponges also cling to some rocks. Crawling slowly through the area are brown spotted nudibranchs, yellow margin nudibranchs, sea lemons, ochre stars, sunflower stars, and leather stars. Curly terebellid worms extend slender white tentacles from crevices in the rock. You can even see a few orange or white plumose anemones. As at other sites in Indian Arm, decorator crabs hang upside down, extending their claws out into the water.

The power plant seen from the south

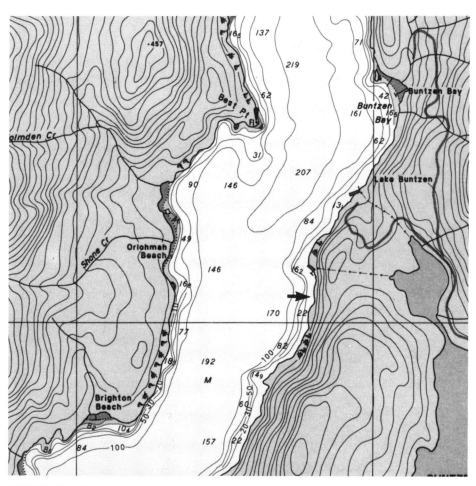

114. Buntzen Island

Boat dive. . .wall drop on west side of island and medium-sloped mud bottom on south tip. . .good site for hovering "in space". . .fair mix of marine life. . .hazards are depth and red jellyfish

Skill level   2 or 3 (see page 11)

Access   Boat dive

Location   Buntzen Island is 1.8 kilometres (1 nautical mile) north of the Buntzen Power Plant in the Buntzen Bay area of central Indian Arm. The dive site is along the western side of the island. Anchorage is available near the south tip of the island in fair holding ground. A tended boat is recommended, especially on windy days. Descend and follow the island.

Hazards   Depth and red jellyfish (see page 12)

Description   Buntzen Island offers a wall dive and a sloped bottom on one site. The west side of the island is a sheer wall with many cracks and crevices to explore. It falls away to depths beyond 100 feet. The south tip is a steep mud bottom with rocky outcroppings. Depths run to 100 feet or more.

Depth and the feeling of weightlessness you get hovering just off the wall are the main attractions on the west side of Buntzen Island. The rock formations are interesting and attract a fair selection of marine life. A highlight is spotting a hairy lithode crab out in the open and seeing its multicoloured legs and body. Various nudibranchs including alabaster, orange spotted, white, yellow margin, and sea lemon inhabit the area. Clusters of calcareous tube worms cover the rock, especially in the deeper sections. Also clinging to the rocks are slippered cucumbers, blood stars, ochre stars, broad base squirts, and limpets. White or grey plumose anemones pop up in places. The medium-sloped south tip of the island is home to sunflower stars, leather stars, California cucumbers, and swimming scallops. Darting everywhere on the site are red and coonstripe shrimp. Gobies lying in the southern part of the site swim away from approaching divers. Copper rockfish hide in crevices or swim lazily about the area. Spindly decorator crabs are found on the rock.

The west side of the island

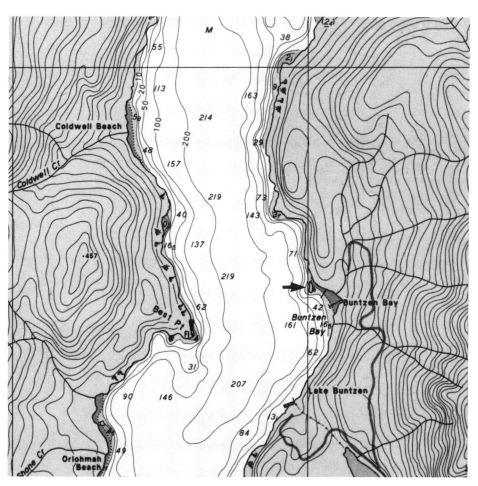

NOT TO BE USED FOR NAVIGATION—see page 9.
Use Canadian chart 3495 for navigation.
For information on obtaining navigational charts, see page 21.

51

115. Boulder Bank

Boat dive. . .shallow with best life 50 feet or less. . .impressive boulders form crevices and overhangs. . .main attractions are nudibranchs and schooling fish. . .hazards are red jellyfish and the occassional boat

Skill level   1 (see page 11)

Access   Boat dive

Location   Boulder Bank is 1.3 kilometres (.7 nautical mile) southeast of Croker Island in northeastern Indian Arm. The dive site is just south of an abandoned gravel operation. Anchorage is available anywhere along the length of the site in shallow water with good holding ground. The site is almost 1 kilometre long, so anchorage position will be determined by the section of the site you wish to explore.

Hazards   Red jellyfish and the occasional boat (see page 12)

Description   Boulder Bank is a pleasant, shallow dive, chock-full of huge boulders forming overhangs and crevices to explore. The gentle to medium sand slope allows divers to choose their depth. Most of the marine life is concentrated in the top 50 feet. Impressive boulders, some 10 to 15 feet high, litter the bottom, attracting a good variety of life. The sand, too, has its attractions. A dive at Boulder Bank can be a long, relaxed affair because of the shallow depth and vast bottom.

The boulders, chiselled in all manner of shapes, spring into sight as you descend. On them you see broad base squirts, stalked hairy sea squirts, and encrusting sponges. Slippered cucumbers and California cucumbers are also found. Clusters of orange and white plumose stand guard over the rocks, while tube-dwelling anemones watch over the sand. One of the most interesting features of Boulder Bank is the variety of types of nudibranchs—common yellow margins, dendronotus diversicolors, janolus fuscus, alabasters, white nudibranchs, and giant nudibranchs—found in the sand and on the boulders. Leather stars, vermilion stars, and ochre stars lie out in the open. Scurrying about the site are decorator, dungeness, and red rock crabs. Hiding in crevices are shy, retiring hairy lithode crabs. Coonstripe shrimp dart under cover when divers approach.

Boulder Bank attracts large schools of fish to its rocky playground. Copper and quillback rockfish, pile perch, and striped perch are readily visible. Small blackeye gobies and eelpouts can also be spotted if you observe the base of the boulders.

The large clearing that marks the northern end of the dive

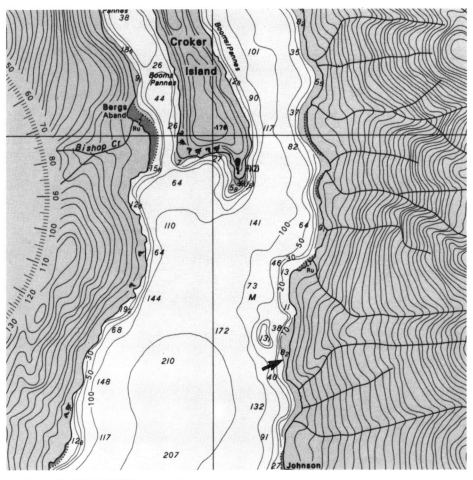

NOT TO BE USED FOR NAVIGATION—see page 9.
Use Canadian chart 3495 for navigation.
For information on obtaining navigational charts, see page 21.

53

116. The Fishbowl/Croker Island South

Boat dive. . .shallow bowl-like depression with silt bottom and scattered rock. . .depths 15 to 25 feet at rim and 50 in bowl. . .schooling fish, nudibranchs, and shrimp highlight marine life. . .hazards are red jellyfish, during summer and fall, and occasional boat traffic

Skill level   1 (see page 11)

Access   Boat dive

Location   Croker Island is 1.9 kilometres (1 nautical mile) south of the mouth of the Indian River in northern Indian Arm. The Fishbowl is at the southeastern tip of the island. The tip is marked by a white circular tower with a white light on top, which flashes after dusk. Fifteen metres west of the tower is a white wooden triangle fixed on a tree. The fishbowl is 10 metres south of the triangle and straight down. Anchorage is available here. Boaters should beware of a large rock that dries at low tide just south of the marker. Those new to the site are advised to proceed with caution.

Hazards   Red jellyfish, during summer and fall, and occasional boat traffic (see page 12)

Description   The Fishbowl derives its name from its scooped, bowl-like shape and its schooling fish. It provides an interesting setting with a controlled environment great for exploration and training. The bowl is approximately 100 metres in diameter. The raised rim is 15 to 25 feet deep and ringed with large rocks. The inner section has a silt bottom with occasional rocky outcroppings and depths to 50 feet. The north end of the bowl is marked underwater by three large logs piled one on top of the other and a large rusting piece of machinery probably discarded by logging operations that once worked on the island.

Inside the Fishbowl is an abundance of life. Tube-dwelling anemones and white sea cucumbers wave gently in the silt. Varieties of sole lie camouflaged on the bottom. Look carefully and you find hairy lithode crabs wedged inside crevices in the rocks. Glued onto the rocks are sea lemons, alabaster nudibranchs, and janolus fuscus nudibranchs. Sea peaches also cling to available rock. Shrimp dart everywhere, leaving wispy trails of disturbed silt. Lingcod, copper rockfish, kelp greenlings, striped perch, and blackeye gobies live around the edge of the bowl. Hovering in the water above the bowl during the summer months are moon jellies, sea gooseberries, and red jellyfish.

The eastern side of the Fishbowl is adjacent to a large rock that reaches the surface on low tides. The face of the rock is packed with hundreds of calcareous tube worms waving coloured fans in the water. The fans withdraw as if on cue when the water around them is disturbed.

The white circular tower and the white triangular marker

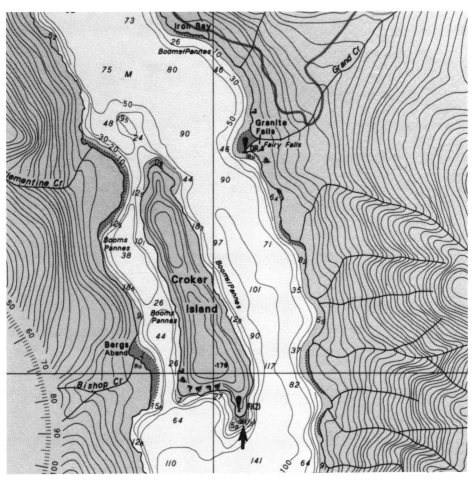

NOT TO BE USED FOR NAVIGATION—see page 9.
Use Canadian chart 3495 for navigation.
For information on obtaining navigational charts, see page 21.

55

117. Croker Island North

Boat dive. . . mud/silt background shows off colours of a good mix of marine life. . . hazards are depth and red jellyfish

Skill level   2 or 3 (see page 11)

Access   Boat dive

Location   Croker Island is 1.9 kilometres (1 nautical mile) south of the mouth of the Indian River in northern Indian Arm. The dive site is the northern tip of the island. Anchorage is available at the tip in shallow water with good holding ground. Descend the anchor line and explore east and west along the tip of the island.

Hazards   Depth and red jellyfish (see page 12)

Description   Croker Island's north tip is similar to dives in northern Howe Sound. The dull grey-brown bottom makes the colours of the resident animals jump out. The bottom at Croker North is steep-sloped mud and silt down to 50 to 60 feet. From there a medium slope runs to 100 feet or more, with silt-covered rocky outcroppings popping up in spots. Some of the outcroppings form dens for marine life to live in.

No one creature is found in profusion, but a great variety of life is here. Plumose anemones dot the area. Tube-dwelling anemones, their tubes exposed in full, live on top of the mud more than in it. Tall graceful sea whips show up bright white against the dull background. Light bulb tunicates, warty tunicates and wrinkled squirts hang from rocks. Crawling through the site are brown spotted nudibranchs and dendronotus rufus. Sea cucumbers are represented by slippered and California varieties. Sea stars are here in the form of sunflower stars, vermilion stars, slime stars, and mud stars. Hiding in the rocky dens are hairy lithode crabs and sailfin sculpins. These shy creatures are quite pretty, especially if they can be coaxed out in the open or made to show themselves off in their dens. Decorator crabs, shrimp, and red rock crabs scuttle about the bottom. Rockfish, lingcod, and sole rest on the mud and silt. In the shallow depths, from the surface to 30 feet, rockweed, kelp, and eelgrass mix with mussels and purple stars.

The north tip of the island seen from the west

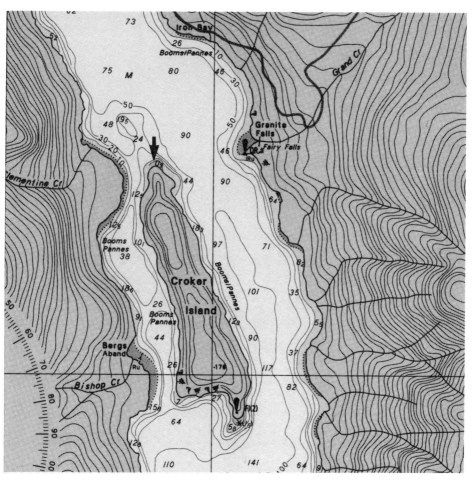

NOT TO BE USED FOR NAVIGATION—see page 9.
Use Canadian chart 3495 for navigation.
For information on obtaining navigational charts, see page 21.

57

118. Rockfish Wall

Boat dive. . .vertical wall to more than 100 feet. . .lots of rockfish and other life. . .great view depending on visibility. . .main hazard is depth

Skill level   3 (see page 11)

Access   Boat dive

Location   Rockfish Wall (don't look for the name on a chart—I made it up) is .9 kilometre (.5 nautical mile) southwest of Croker Island light in northwestern Indian Arm. To find the dive site, look for the first large vertical wall southwest of Croker Island with large splashes of yellow high above the waterline. Anchor to the north of the wall in the small bay or use a tended boat. Enter at the north end of the wall and move south.

Hazards   Depth (see page 12)

Description   Rockfish Wall allows divers to hang weightless in the water while viewing a vertical world of sea creatures. The wall has an impressive flat face similar to its above-water extension, with a large boulder-strewn ledge in 50 to 60 feet on the northern section. The base of the wall runs to 100 feet or more before meeting a steep sand bottom. Cracks and crevices are present and bear investigation.

Rockfish Wall is an awesome sight on days with good visibility. You can see from top to bottom and recognize some of the marine life far off. Even from a distance, California cucumbers, sunflower stars, and patches of yellow encrusting sponge are clear. Moving along the wall face, you see vermilion stars, morning sunstars, and ochre stars. Lampshells shut tight and rotate their shells upwards when the water around them is disturbed. Wrinkled sea squirts, broad base sea squirts, warty tunicates, and slippered cucumbers protrude from the rock. Terebellid worms extend long white tentacles along the surface of the wall. Crawling slowly along are brown spotted, white, and alabaster nudibranchs. Look carefully into a crevice and you find hairy lithode crabs retreating into the darkness. Scuttling about in the open are hordes of decorator crabs and kelp crabs. Calcareous tube worms are found in deep and shallow sections. Schools of shiner and striped perch hover in the vicinity. Rockfish are everywhere. If you look out in the open, in crevices, or even under rocks, you are likely to spot quillbacks and coppers on their own or in small groups.

The flat face of the wall

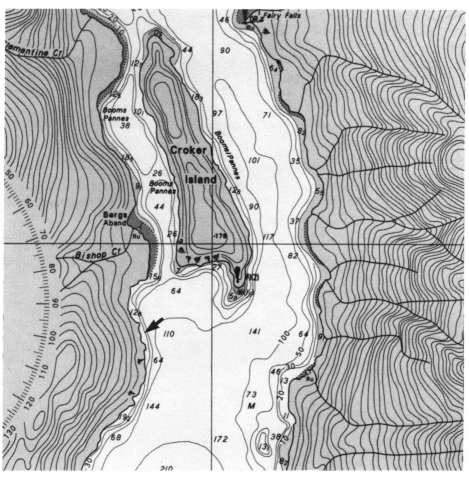

119. Powell Bay

Boat dive. . .interesting geography, including fissure and overhang. . .can go deep very quickly. . .good mix of marine life. . .main hazard is depth

Skill level   4 (see page 11)

Access   Boat dive

Location   Powell Bay (a name I made up) is located 1.3 kilometres (.7 nautical mile) southwest of the southern tip of Croker Island in northwestern Indian Arm. The bay is a small steep-sided indentation in the coastline immediately south of Rockfish Wall (see page 58). Anchorage is difficult for even small boats, because the bottom slopes away at a very steep angle. A tended boat is advised.

Hazards   Depth (see page 12)

Description   Powell Bay is a deep dive with interesting geography. The bay appears to have been carved out by a creek long ago. Underwater, an impressive drop-off is punctuated by small rocky ledges, a fissure, and a large overhang that is just big enough to allow a diver to wriggle in up to his or her head and shoulders. Down the centre of the bay is a steep slope made up of small rocks with the odd boulder. You can go deep in a hurry at this site or enjoy the view from a shallower depth when the visibility is good.

Since the site is compact, a leisurely dive allows you to enjoy the geography and the marine life scattered on the rock. The shallow areas of the bay are draped in long, flowing kelp leaves, some of which play host to kelp-encrusting bryozoans. Hairy lithode crabs and decorator crabs lie in crevices or out in the open. Sea stars are represented by leather, sunflower, ochre, vermilion, morning, and slime varieties. California cucumbers and white nudibranchs crawl slowly along the rock. Orange encrusting sponge, cream-coloured sponge, coralene algae, wrinkled squirts, broad base squirts, false Pacific jingle shells, and orange cup corals cling tenaciously to the bottom. Calcareous tube worms and curly terebellid worms are also found. Two unexpected inhabitants of this rocky area are sole and clams. Just visiting, I guess. Flashes of black and yellow are provided by copper rockfish.

The bay

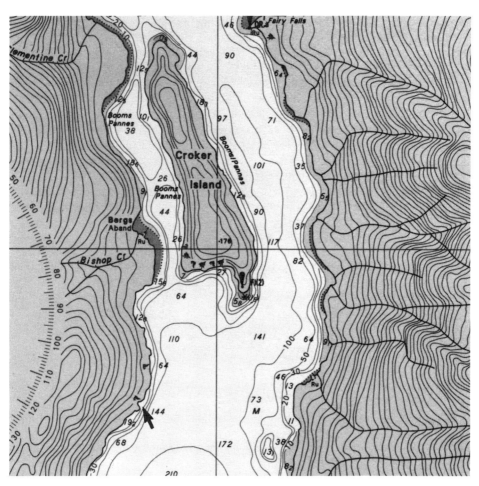

NOT TO BE USED FOR NAVIGATION—see page 9.
Use Canadian chart 3495 for navigation.
For information on obtaining navigational charts, see page 21.

61

120. Best Point

Boat dive. . .steep drops, walls, ledges with boulders. . .good mix of marine life and some man-made objects. . .hazards are depth, red jellyfish, and float lines

Skill level 2 or 3 (see page 11)

Access Boat dive

Location Best Point is 7.4 kilometres (3.8 nautical miles) north of Deep Cove in central Indian Arm. It is marked by a white circular tower with a white light that flashes after dusk. Anchorage is available just off the point, but the holding ground is poor. A tended boat is advised. Enter south of the point, explore the north side of the small bay, and then move north along the point.

Hazards Depth, red jellyfish, and float lines (see page 12)

Description Best Point is a fun site to explore because of its changing geography. It is a world of walls, ledges, and steep slopes with interesting man-made and natural attractions. The area around the point drops sharply from the shore to 30 to 40 feet. From there, walls and intermittent ledges in the central and northern sections and steep-sloped sand in the south continue the drop into 100 feet or more. The largest ledges, in the central section at 70 to 80 feet, have large boulders. The northern limit of the dive is marked by a series of rusty cables anchoring docks and floats. The rocks in water deeper than 50 feet have a light dusting of silt and crushed shell.

The shallow rock at Best Point is draped in brown kelp leaves and speckled with keyhole limpets and false Pacific jingle shells. Descend a bit deeper and you see sunflower stars, false ochre stars, morning sunstars, and California cucumbers. Look carefully at the rock to glimpse a buffalo sculpin blended in with its surroundings. Also hiding in the area are sturgeon poachers and grunt sculpins. Clinging to the rocks are red slippered cucumbers, fiery red alabaster nudibranchs, and bright pink coralene algae. Blood stars and vermilion stars are found in spots. Standing guard over the site are tall orange and white plumose anemones and squat grey plumose. Dotting the rocks at various depths are brown lampshells, which close tight when the water around them is disturbed. Thousands of coonstripe shrimp and light brown shrimp peer out from crevices in the rock or dart over the ledges. Circling over the area are quillback rockfish, striped perch, and shiner perch. You can even see tube-dwelling anemones and short-spined stars living in the silt on the ledges.

In addition to its natural attractions, Best Point has some man-made objects, including a bicycle, a couple of barrels, some rusty cables that are slowly being covered by grey plumose anemones and mussels, and several unidentifiable rusting metal lumps.

The white circular tower of the point seen from the south

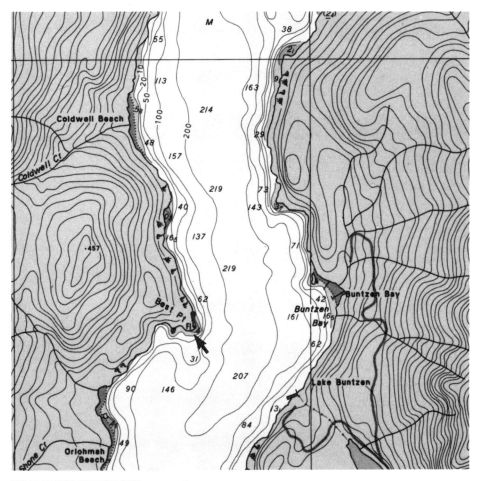

NOT TO BE USED FOR NAVIGATION—see page 9.
Use Canadian chart 3495 for navigation.
For information on obtaining navigational charts, see page 21.

63

121. Brighton Cliffs

Boat dive. . .steep slope or wall with small ledges. . .depths to 120 feet or more. . .life at all levels. . .hazards are depth and red jellyfish

Skill level   3 (see page 11)

Access   Boat dive

Location   Brighton Cliffs are 4.5 kilometres (2.4 nautical miles) north of Deep Cove in the Brighton Beach area of central Indian Arm. The dive site is the 800-metre-long set of cliffs north of the Brighton Beach community on the west side of the Arm. Anchorage is available just inside the bay right against the shore. On days with a southerly wind it is best to have a tended boat. Enter at the southern end of the cliffs and move north.

Hazards   Depth and red jellyfish (see page 12)

Description   Brighton Cliffs is a deep dive that allows you to hover ''in space'' or move close in and investigate the slope. The steep, rocky wall resembles its above-water extension. Small ledges pop out at various points along the wall. A light covering of silt and crushed shell lies on top of the slope and the ledges. Depths at the base of the wall run to more than 120 feet.

Brighton Cliffs is a good spot to explore as a multilevel dive by heading out deep and returning shallow. The deep water provides habitat for clusters of calcareous tube worms, slippered cucumbers, and blood stars. Some very large lingcod lie brooding on the rock. Move up to medium depths of 40 to 80 feet and you see tan and orange cup corals, the odd orange or white plumose anemone, some white tipped anemones, and swimming anemones. Also in this area are broad base squirts, glassy sea squirts, terebellid worms, California cucumbers, yellow margin nudibranchs, Hudson's dorids, and a ''mystery'' nudibranch similar to a tritonia festiva but red at the ends and white in the middle.

The shallowest sections of Brighton Cliffs, from 40 feet to the surface, are home to kelp, sea lettuce, and a number of different sea creatures. Transparent sea squirts, limpets, brown spotted nudibranchs, alabaster nudibranchs, and flabellina salmonacea live on the rocks. Painted greenlings, scaleyhead sculpins, and dungeness crabs move up and down along the bottom. At all levels of the site, you see lingcod, quillback rockfish, decorator crabs, and shrimp.

The cliffs seen from the south

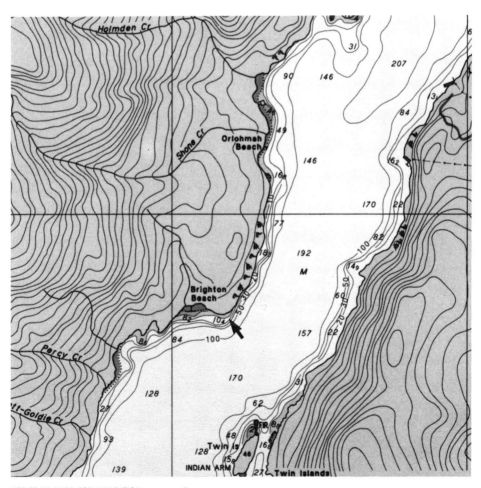

NOT TO BE USED FOR NAVIGATION—see page 9.
Use Canadian chart 3495 for navigation.
For information on obtaining navigational charts, see page 21.

65

122. Lone Rock Point (also called Woodlands)

Shore dive. . .easy access via dock. . .walls, steps, and slopes make up the bottom . . .shrimp abound. . .interesting miniature life in shallow water. . .hazards are boat traffic, depth, and red jellyfish

Skill level   2 or 3 (see page 11)

Access   Shore dive

Location   Lone Rock Point is in the Woodlands area north of Deep Cove in southeastern Indian Arm. From the Second Narrows Bridge, take the Mount Seymour Parkway exit. Follow the Parkway to Mount Seymour Road and turn left. Just before the gates to Mount Seymour Park, turn right onto Indian River Road. Follow it to Indian River Creek and turn right. Indian River Creek twists and turns a narrow path through the rainforest and ends at a cul de sac. Unload gear there, and park a short way up the hill. Take the path to the Woodlands public dock. The dive site is northeast of the dock and is marked by a white circular tower with a green band at the top and a green light that flashes after dusk. Snorkel from the dock to the marker, descend, and move east and then north.

Hazards   Boat traffic, depth, and red jellyfish (see page 12)

Description   Lone Rock Point provides easy access and a varied bottom for divers to explore. As you descend at the marker, you come upon a small wall full of sunflower stars. The bottom soon drops away in a series of rocky steps to a boulder-strewn sand slope in 30 to 40 feet of water. Move north around a small corner and you are on a large wall face that drops past 100 feet very quickly.

Shrimp are the most common inhabitants of Lone Rock Point. They cover the walls, slopes, and steps. Decorator and red rock crabs scuttle up and down. Row upon row of small acorn barnacles adhere to the rock. Yellow margin nudibranchs, light bulb tunicates, glassy sea squirts, lined chitons, calcareous tube worms, and orange and white plumose anemones are also glued to the large wall. Sea lemons, alabaster nudibranchs, orange cucumbers, and California cucumbers can be seen. At the northern end of the wall is a scattering of cinder blocks that provide homes for red rock crabs and grunt sculpins.

The shallow section of the dive, 25 feet and less, is a miniature land of tiny sunflower stars, mini decorator crabs, small rock crabs, and little hermit crabs in tiny shells. Scaleyhead sculpins, CO sole, and sandy sole are also in shallow water.

Wheelchair access   The path and the ramp leading to the dock are steep and should be negotiated with care. Diving at high tide helps overcome problems with the ramp.

The white circular tower with green top band seen from the dock

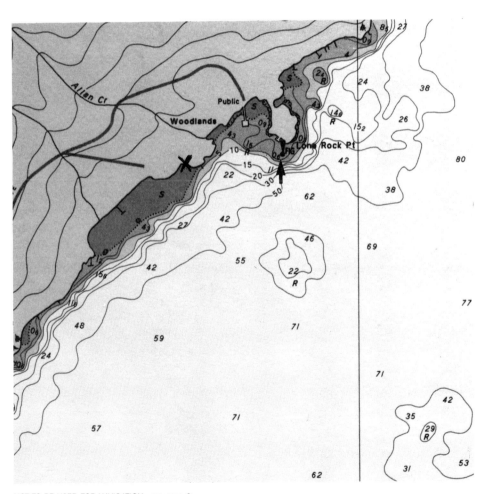

NOT TO BE USED FOR NAVIGATION—see page 9.
Use Canadian chart 3495 for navigation.
For information on obtaining navigational charts, see page 21.

67

123. Grey Rocks Island (also called Strathcona)

Shore dive. . .close to Vancouver. . .depth to 100 feet on sloping rock with ledges and small walls. . .good marine life mix with two white plumose colonies a highlight. . .hazards are boat traffic, current in the bay, red jellyfish, and depth

Skill level 2 or 3 (see page 11)

Access Shore dive

Location Grey Rocks Island is in the Strathcona area north of Cates Park and south of Deep Cove in southeastern Indian Arm. From the Second Narrows Bridge, take the Deep Cove exit onto Dollarton Highway and drive past Cates Park. Dollarton turns into Deep Cove Road. Take the first right onto Strathcona Road. Follow the road .7 kilometre to the water. Small parking lots at the head of the dock and to the right provide parking for five or six cars. Gear up and snorkel or (at very low tides) walk to Grey Rocks Island. Descend on the southwest side and move out around the island.

Hazards Boat traffic, current in the bay, red jellyfish, and depth (see page 12)

Description Grey Rocks Island has a quick shore entry and interesting marine life on the snorkel and the dive. The shallow bay separating the island and the dock is home to sea gooseberries, moon jellies, pile perch, hooded nudibranchs, and bubble shells, which grow on and around the waving eelgrass.

Descend the southwestern side of the island. The rock-strewn sand bottom holds kelp, sea lettuce, purple stars, sunflower stars, and shiner perch. The bottom slopes gently down as you move along the island. A rocky reef on the southeast tip of the island drops from the surface to 45 feet before giving way to a sand slope. A small wall on the face of the reef is coated with grey, blue, and orange sunflower stars and hops with thousands of shrimp.

On the rocky slope of the island's east side are two large colonies of white plumose anemones, one at 35 feet and the other at 50 feet. Clusters of barnacles packed together wave frantically in the water, trapping food. Yellow encrusting sponge, false Pacific jingle shells, giant barnacles, ostrich plume hydroids, California cucumbers, alabaster nudibranchs, yellow margin nudibranchs, striped sunstars, and decorator crabs are found. Several large yellow-coloured crimson anemones grow on the slope. Calcareous tube worms inhabit the deeper waters, which run deeper than 100 feet along the rocks. Solitary sculpins and schools of tube snouts and quillback rockfish move about the area.

The north side of the island is mainly shallow flat sand littered with pieces of wood and metal disposed of in the water. A few sole, short-spined stars, elegant burrowing anemones, and slime feather dusters pop out of the sand.

Wheelchair access Easy access to the beach, although you may get a bit dirty at low tide when moving through the bay.

The island with the dock in the foreground

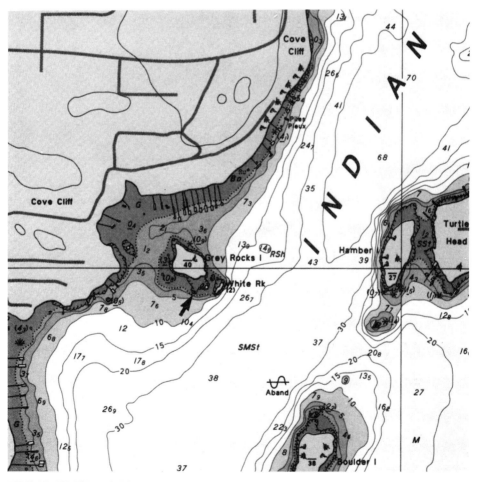

NOT TO BE USED FOR NAVIGATION—see page 9.
Use Canadian chart 3495 for navigation.
For information on obtaining navigational charts, see page 21.

69

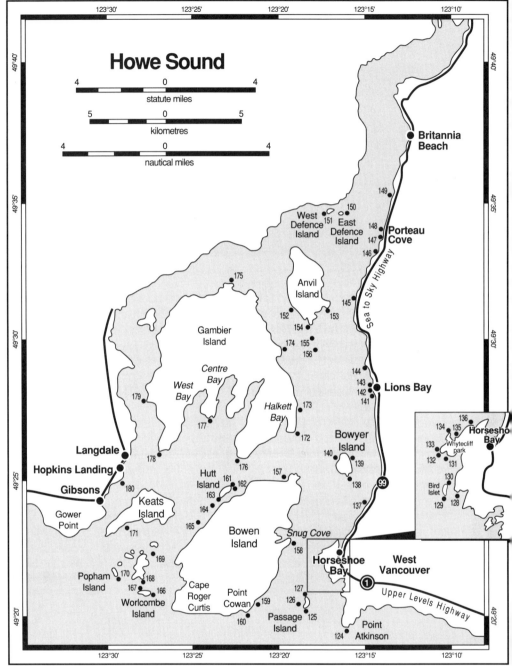

Howe Sound

statute miles

kilometres

nautical miles

Britannia Beach

Porteau Cove

Sea to Sky Highway

West Defence Island

East Defence Island

Anvil Island

Gambier Island

Centre Bay

West Bay

Halkett Bay

Lions Bay

Langdale

Hopkins Landing

Gibsons

Gower Point

Keats Island

Hutt Island

Bowyer Island

Bowen Island

Snug Cove

Horseshoe Bay

West Vancouver

Popham Island

Worlcombe Island

Cape Roger Curtis

Point Cowan

Passage Island

Point Atkinson

Upper Levels Highway

Horseshoe Bay

Whytecliff park

Bird Islet

Part Three: Diving in Howe Sound

Framed by the scenic Coast Mountains, Howe Sound stretches 43 kilometres (23.5 nautical miles) south from the mouth of the Squamish River to a line joining Point Atkinson in West Vancouver and Gower Point near Gibsons. The beautiful mountain views and picturesque islands a short trip west of Vancouver make the area a favourite destination. Divers find many beautiful views easily accessible in the subsurface realm of the Sound.

Howe Sound is divided into two distinct regions. The northern, or upper, Sound is a fjord 3 kilometres (1.6 nautical miles) wide and 17 kilometres (9 nautical miles) long that runs between the mouth of the Squamish River and Anvil Island. A relatively shallow sill, 115 feet deep, running from the Defence Islands to Porteau Cove is a partial barrier to water moving north and provides shore access for divers in the shallow bays of the Porteau area. Many of the other dives are accessible by boat or can be reached through sometimes steep and rocky scuba hikes. Dotted with islands large and small, lower Howe Sound is a much wider area. It is an average 20 kilometres (11 nautical miles) across and 26 kilometres (14 nautical miles) long. The steep mountains and many islands provide the lower Sound with a variety of dive sites. Shallow bays of silt, mud, and sand; rocky reefs; pinnacles; and steep sloping rock walls can all be found in the area. Access to many of the better dives is by boat, although there are also many excellent shore dives.

The shores of Howe Sound are served by a series of well-marked and well-maintained roadways. The southeastern shores between Point Atkinson and Horseshoe Bay are reached by roads branching off Marine Drive, which leads through West Vancouver from the First Narrows Bridge. The Upper Levels Highway, Highway 1/99, which runs from the Second Narrows Bridge to Horseshoe Bay, can be used to bypass Marine Drive, a slower, more urban roadway. At Horseshoe Bay, Highway 99, called the Sea to Sky Highway, begins its winding journey north to Squamish. Access to shore dives north of Horseshoe Bay is via this highway. Shore dives on Bowen Island are reached via the Horseshoe Bay–Snug Cove ferry run and then the road system of the island. Some of the roads are quite rough and are really no more than gravel paths.

The Howe Sound area has many facilities for divers. There are grocery stores, restaurants, telephones, and gas stations in Gibsons, Squamish, Horseshoe Bay, and West Vancouver, and there are corner grocery stores in Lions Bay, Britannia Beach, and Snug Cove on Bowen Island. Porteau Cove is a very comfortable place to dive, with change rooms, washrooms, indoor and outdoor showers, picnic facilities, a telephone, and steps leading to the water. Diving attractions are well marked and maps on shore provide an explanation of the site layout.

Divers with boats also have many facilities available. There are marine parks in Halkett Bay on Gambier Island and Plumper Cove on Keats Island and gas barges at the marinas at Gibsons, Snug Cove, and Horseshoe Bay. On the mainland, temporary moorage is available at Caulfield Cove near Point Atkinson, at Horseshoe Bay, at Hopkins Landing just south of Langdale, and at Gibsons. On the islands, temporary moorage is available at New Brighton in Thornbrough Bay on Gambier Island, at Halkett Bay (dinghies only) on Gambier, at Eastbourne and Plumper Cove on Keats Island, and at Galbraith Bay and Snug Cove on Bowen Island. Boat launch ramps are available at several locations on the mainland and on Keats Island. Mainland boat launches on the east side of Howe Sound include West Bay in West Vancouver, Sewell's Marina in Horseshoe Bay, Sunset Beach Marina, Newman Creek Marina, Lions Bay Marina, and Porteau Cove.

124. Point Atkinson

Boat or shore, although shore access is a hike. . .rocky rolling shore continues into 30 to 65 feet with sloped sand base. . .good variety of marine life. . .hazards are boats and wind

Skill level   1 or 2 (see page 11)

Access   Boat or shore dive

Location   Point Atkinson is the southeastern tip of Howe Sound. It is marked by a white and red lighthouse with several white buildings in the immediate area. The dive site is along the rocky shore at the very south tip of the point. Anchorage is available in the small shallow bay to the west of the point. Care should be exercised when anchoring, as this area is open to winds from all directions and the water is frequently choppy. As a shore dive, Point Atkinson can be reached by turning onto Beacon Lane from Marine Drive in West Vancouver, parking in the lot for Lighthouse Park, following the path to the lighthouse, and then continuing along forest trails to the west side of the lighthouse. Total walking distance is approximately 1 kilometre. Carts, pack mules, or Sherpa guides are recommended as this is a long trek down to the water and an even longer one back up the hill to the parking lot after the dive.

Hazards   Boat traffic and wind-generated surge (see page 12)

Description   Point Atkinson is a great introduction to the diving found in Howe Sound. The sloped rolling shore is mirrored underwater to a depth of 30 to 65 feet. An occasional crevice shelters some animals, but most of the marine life lies out in the open. At the base of the rock is a gentle to medium sloped sand bottom punctuated by the odd boulder.

The viewing begins as soon as you leave the surface. Huge beds of green sea urchins crowd the upper rock. Sea lettuce, bull kelp, leafy kelp, mussels, barnacles, and purple stars live in the shallow water. A little deeper, leafy hornmouths, leather stars, short-spined stars, striped sunstars, and California cucumbers appear. At various depths down to 60 feet you find slime stars, sunflower stars, morning sunstars, red and purple urchins, orange sea cucumbers, glassy sea squirts, and orange tennis ball sponges. Nudibranchs are represented by white, opalescent, lemon peel, janolus fuscus, and flabellina salmonecea varieties. On the western side of the point, an octopus lies in a crevice in 45 feet of water. Coonstripe shrimp dart back and forth like underwater grasshoppers. Large cabezons, great sculpins, scaleyhead sculpins, kelp greenlings, and schools of tube snouts also call the point home. In the sand at the base of the point are sea pens and clams.

Wheelchair access   Not recommended as a shore dive. The rocky trails near the water are impassable for chairs.

The lighthouse and buildings seen from the south

NOT TO BE USED FOR NAVIGATION—see page 9.
Use Canadian chart 3526 for navigation.
For information on obtaining navigational charts, see page 21.

73

125. Passage Island South Islet

Boat dive, simple and shallow with sand bottom all around and some rocks and boulders to the south. . .depths reach 70 feet. . .good variety of life including nudibranchs and octopus. . .hazards are boat traffic and wind

Skill level   1 or 2 (see page 11)

Access   Boat dive

Location   Passage Island is 2.8 kilometres (1.5 nautical miles) west of Point Atkinson in southeastern Howe Sound. The dive site is around the islet at the southern tip of the island. Anchorage is available in shallow water on the east side of the islet. Caution should be exercised when anchoring, because of the submerged rocks northeast of the islet. The area's exposure to winds from Georgia Strait may also make anchoring difficult. Descend and move south and then around the islet.

Hazards   Boat traffic and wind (see page 12)

Description   Passage Island South Islet is a shallow, pleasant dive a short boat ride from Vancouver. The eastern side of the islet has a flat, sandy bottom averaging 20 feet in depth. When you move south, rock and boulder fields appear. The depth averages 40 to 50 feet and reaches 70 feet maximum. The west side of the islet becomes shallow as you head north; the north tip is dry at very low tides.

East of the islet, the sand bottom holds a wealth of clam shells and siphons. Dungeness crabs, sea pens, and short-spined stars are also found. Long, thin bay pipefish hover above the sand. Some swim close to motionless divers and wrap their bodies around outstretched arms. Along the rocky foreshore of the islet, large beds of green urchins, kelp, mussels, acorn barnacles, lined chitons, and purple stars compete for space.

Descending along the islet's south side to the boulder fields, divers see red shrimp, coonstripe shrimp, crimson anemones, Pacific pink scallops, pink mouth hydroids, purple and red sea urchins, and kelp greenlings. A large variety of nudibranchs including janolus fuscus, yellow margin, white, striped, brown spotted, and opalescent live among the rocks. Two octopuses have set up dens in crevices. The west side of the islet is home to lightbulb tunicates, orange and mottled slime stars, blood stars, morning sunstars, leather stars, scaleyhead sculpins, and schooling perch. Beds of green urchins are seen in the shallow waters of the northwest side of the islet.

The east side of the south islet

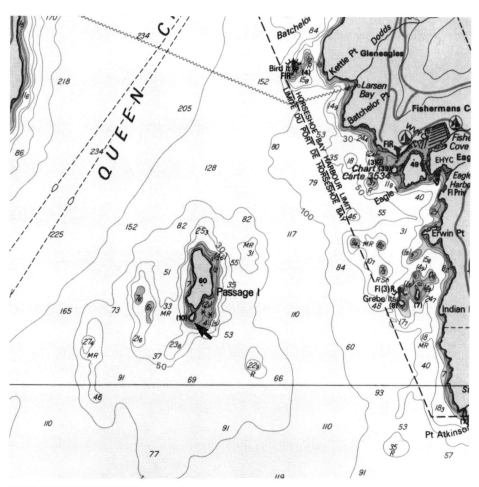

NOT TO BE USED FOR NAVIGATION—see page 9.
Use Canadian chart 3526 for navigation.
For information on obtaining navigational charts, see page 21.

75

126. Passage Island Reefs

Boat dive, one of the best in Howe Sound . . . two rocky pinnacles rising to within 20 feet of the surface from several hundred feet . . . very interesting geography and marine life . . . hazards are boat traffic, current, wind, and depth

Skill level   2 or 3 (see page 11)

Access   Boat dive

Location   Passage Island Reefs are 400 to 600 metres west of Passage Island in southeastern Howe Sound. To find them, drive due west away from the south tip of the island or the off-white house with the flared roof (see photo) and watch your depth sounder carefully. When it reads in the 30-to-60-foot range, prepare to drop anchor. Drop an anchor or a marker, preferably in 60 to 70 feet of water, as the shallower depths are covered in life and provide poor holding ground. This area is open to winds from the south and west, which may make anchoring difficult. Follow the line down and explore.

Hazards   Boat traffic, current, wind, and depth (see page 12)

Description   Marine life and geography compete for divers' attention at one of Howe Sound's best dives. The twin pinnacles rise seemingly from nowhere to sit 20 feet from the surface of the water. Rocky ridges form miniature canyons for divers to explore. Steep drop-offs and flat rocky plains can be found in this wonderfully varied site. Cracks, crevices, and boulders are everywhere, enticing divers to peek in. Divers can choose their depth based on training and experience.

The shallower areas at Passage Reefs are flat rocky table tops packed solid with white plumose anemones big and small. Slightly deeper, ridges and canyons begin, and zoanthids, giant barnacles, calcareous tube worms, green sea urchins, and yellow boring sponges coat the rocks. Sea pens, rock scallops, swimming scallops, brittle stars, white and orange sea cucumbers, lampshells, sea peaches, and glassy sea squirts have their own areas. Large lingcod, quillback rockfish, and kelp greenlings swim close to the rocks.

In deeper water, you see sprawling long ray stars, tall orange and white plumose, and large purple urchins. Cloud sponges and chimney sponges, some only 60 feet deep, shine out of the rocky depths. Divers who observe carefully are rewarded with the sight of a Puget Sound king crab. Coonstripe shrimp are also abundant on the reef.

The view when anchored on the reefs

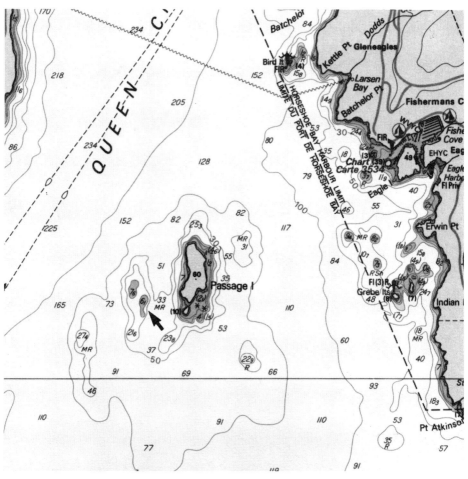

NOT TO BE USED FOR NAVIGATION—see page 9.
Use Canadian chart 3526 for navigation.
For information on obtaining navigational charts, see page 21.

77

127. Passage Island North

Boat dive. . .shallow boulder and rock slopes. . .ledges and walls to depths of 100 feet or more. . .each bottom type has its own marine life. . .hazards are depth and boats

Skill level 2 or 3 (see page 11)

Access Boat dive

Location Passage Island is 2.8 kilometres (1.5 nautical miles) west of Point Atkinson in southeastern Howe Sound. The dive site is on the north tip of the island. Anchorage is available near the small bay to the east of the tip of the island. The site is open to winds from the north, which can make anchoring difficult. A tended boat is advised on windy days. Descend on the eastern side of the tip of the island and move west.

Hazards Boat traffic and depth (see page 12)

Description Passage Island north is a dive with life at all levels. At the northern tip of the island, rock and boulder slopes descend into 20 to 30 feet of water. A sandy ledge descends to 55 feet, where an intriguing wall drops straight into 100 feet or more. To the west of the island's tip, a long wall drops from near the surface to 60 feet before meeting a steep sand bottom. East of the tip, rocks and boulders slope into 20 to 30 feet and then give way to sloping sand.

The rocky shallows of the northern tip and eastern side of Passage Island are a perfect home for beds of small green sea urchins. Large kelp leaves and orange finger sponges also thrive in this spot. The deeper waters of the ledge and north wall support clumps of large orange and white plumose anemones and huge red and purple sea urchins. Pink and red crimson anemones, yellowy lacy bryozoans, colourful shrimp, and bright orange sea pens also live in the deep sections of the site. Colonies of sea firs and yellow boring sponge are found. In the very deep sections, past 100 feet, cloud sponges and rose stars are common. Hiding in rocky dens are small schools of copper rockfish. Solitary kelp greenlings retreat from approaching divers.

The western wall presents another mix of marine life. Colonies of zoanthids coat sections of the wall. Orange cup corals, giant barnacles, sea lemons, white cucumbers, morning sunstars, slime stars, and rose stars cling to the rock face. Painted brittle stars wave slender arms out from cracks in the wall. Blue top snails move slowly over the rock. Red Irish lords lie still, blending in with their surroundings. Deep in some crevices, small heart crabs can be glimpsed.

The north tip of the island seen from the northeast

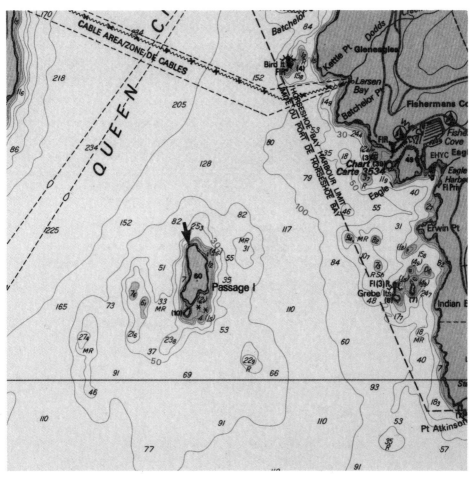

NOT TO BE USED FOR NAVIGATION—see page 9.
Use Canadian chart 3526 for navigation.
For information on obtaining navigational charts, see page 21.

79

128. Larsen Bay—Kettle Point

Shore dive. . .shallow rock and sand entry with shallow wall on north side. . .depth to 50 feet. . .life in sand and on wall. . .good site for getting away from the crowds at Whytecliff. . .hazard is boat traffic at the end of the point

Skill level   1 (see page 11)

Access   Shore dive

Location   Larsen Bay is between Point Atkinson and Whytecliff Park in southeastern Howe Sound. Take the Upper Levels Highway to the Eagleridge exit. Follow Eagleridge down to Marine Drive and turn left. The first right is Gleneagles Drive. Follow Gleneagles to a small gravel parking lot in front of a tennis court. Walk down the path to Larsen Bay, enter at the shore, and move west along the northern side of the bay.

Hazards   Boat traffic at the end of the point (see page 12)

Description   Larsen Bay is something simple and something different for those looking for a dive in the Whytecliff area. An easy entry over small rocks turns into a sand bottom in 10 to 15 feet of water. The north side of the bay is a steep drop to 40 or 50 feet maximum depth. Rocks, boulders, and small walls provide homes for a large variety of marine life. The medium-sloped sand bottom at the base of the drop also merits a look.

The rocks in the entry portion of the bay are covered with barnacles, purple stars, and sea lettuce. Clams, eelgrass, and sea lettuce are common in the shallow sand. Along the northern section of the bay, the rock formations provide an endless series of holes, cracks, and crevices for divers to explore. Broad leaf kelp coated in encrusting bryozoans covers the upper sections. Mussels, sea lettuce, sea peaches, and painted stars are also found. Slighty deeper, false Pacific jingle shells, lined chitons, and coralene algae dot the rocks. Bright orange cucumbers, California cucumbers, sunflower stars, morning sunstars, glassy sea squirts, and green urchins appear in spots. Sea lemons, yellow margin nudibranchs, giant barnacles, and yellow boring sponge also live among the rocks.

The steep sand slope at the base of the rocks is home to tube-dwelling anemones, short-spined stars, and thousands of brittle stars. Swift-moving blackeye gobies swim for cover when divers approach. Schools of tube snouts and striped perch move through all levels. Kelp greenlings, sculpins, and quillback rockfish also swim through the area.

Wheelchair access   The hill from the parking lot to the beach must be negotiated with care. Once on the beach, you are only a short distance from the water.

Kettle Point seen from across the beach

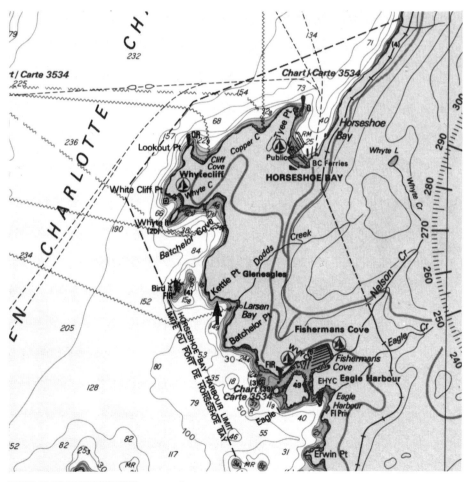

NOT TO BE USED FOR NAVIGATION—see page 9.
Use Canadian chart 3526 for navigation.
For information on obtaining navigational charts, see page 21.

81

129. Bird Islet and South Reef

Boat dive. . . reef on southern section of dive is deep on west side, shallow on east, and coated with white plumose on top. . . urchins are everywhere. . . islet has shallow rock wall with sloped sand . . . octopus hiding in the rock . . . hazards are boat traffic, current, and depth

Skill level   2 or 3 (see page 11)

Access   Boat dive

Location   Bird Islet is located 4.1 kilometres (2.2 nautical miles) north of Point Atkinson in southeastern Howe Sound. It is marked on the southwest corner by a white circular tower with a red band on top and a red light that flashes after dusk. Boaters should anchor to the east of the reef and south of the islet, where the sand bottom provides good holding ground in relatively shallow water. The reef is shallow at low tides, so boaters should drive around it rather than over it. Descend the anchor line and move south around the tip of the reef and then north.

Hazards   Boat traffic, current, and depth (see page 12)

Description   Deep or shallow, the view is excellent at Bird Islet and its rocky southern reef. The eastern side of the reef is a small wall with a base that varies in depth from 15 to 60 feet and averages about 30. Large purple, giant red, and small green sea urchins sit in groups at the base. Sea stars, kelp greenlings, rock scallops, leafy hornmouths, and clams are found here. Hermit crabs move about.

The southern extent of the reef is marked by rocks and boulders that give way to a bottom of sand and broken shell. Flatfish inhabit the wall and the sand. Painted stars, urchins, giant barnacles, alabaster nudibranchs, calcareous tube worms, and blue top snails have rock resting places. Lingcod and striped perch swim on all sides of the reef.

The west side of the reef takes you along a bumpy wall where depth is limited only by experience, as the bottom is hundreds of feet down. The top of the reef is 12 to 20 feet deep and runs due south of the marker. A continuous blanket of stubby white plumose anemones coats several hundred feet of its length, while beds of small green sea urchins cling to the remaining exposed rocks.

The north section of the reef continues the wall face of the west and joins it to the shallow wall of the east as the reef makes the transition to islet. Sea pens, urchins, and a large octopus make the island worth a circuit.

The marker seen from the south

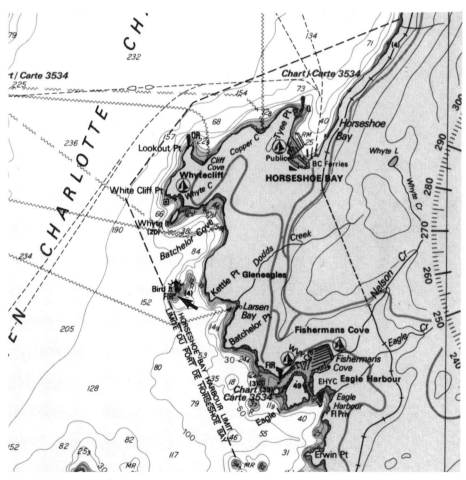

NOT TO BE USED FOR NAVIGATION—see page 9.
Use Canadian chart 3526 for navigation.
For information on obtaining navigational charts, see page 21.

83

130. Bird Islet Pinnacle

Boat dive. . . rocky pinnacle with depths to 60 feet and to 100 or more at extreme south end. . . great invertebrate life but few fish. . . hazards are boat traffic, current, and depth on south side

Skill level 2 or 3 (see page 11)

Access Boat dive

Location Bird Islet Pinnacle is 4.1 kilometres (2.2 nautical miles) north of Point Atkinson in southeastern Howe Sound. It is near the white circular tower with the red top band that marks Bird Islet. The pinnacle is 50 metres northeast of the islet. On very low tides, it rises to 6 to 8 feet from the surface of the water. Anchorage is available to the east of the pinnacle, where the sand bottom provides good holding ground. Descend the anchor line and circle the pinnacle.

Hazards Boat traffic, current, and depth on south side (see page 12)

Description Bird Islet Pinnacle is an undulating rocky reef that displays life like a botanical garden. Large fields of white plumose anemones and colonies of green and purple urchins spring instantly to the eye. Clumps of giant barnacles covered in orange encrusting sponge push purple tentacles through the water in search of food. California sea cucumbers are everywhere.

The north end of the pinnacle drops 60 feet to a gently sloped sand bottom. Sea firs, green urchins, and plumose anemones cover the rocks. Tube-dwelling anemones are in the sand. Move east and the bottom becomes shallow and loose rocks and boulders appear. Among the rocks are swimming scallops, spindle whelks, Oregon hairy tritons, leafy hornmouths, blue top snails, lampshells, zoanthids, and yellow boring sponge. Large orange ribbon worms and tiny orange cup corals can also be found.

The south section of the pinnacle drops away steeply, reaching depths of over 100 feet before sand and silt take over. Some green urchin colonies, calcareous tube worms, orange plumose anemones, and whelks inhabit this area.

The pinnacle has surprisingly few fish. The odd lingcod or painted greenling lies on the rocks peering about. On the west side, the pinnacle shallows to 15 to 25 feet where it joins Bird Islet. The bottom is mainly sand and broken shell with tube-dwelling anemones, brittle stars, and sea pens.

The islet and its marker seen from the north

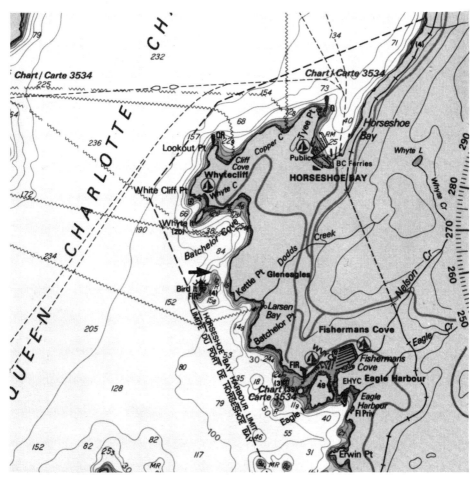

NOT TO BE USED FOR NAVIGATION—see page 9.
Use Canadian chart 3526 for navigation.
For information on obtaining navigational charts, see page 21.

85

131. Whyte Islet

Shore dive. . .series of ledges runs past 100 feet on north side. . .sand and rock slope west. . .shallow rock and sand south and east. . .life varies with bottom. . .plumose beds at west end, octopus. . .hazards are boat traffic, current, and fishing line

Skill level   2 or 3 (see page 11)

Access   Shore dive

Location   Whyte Islet is on the southern side of Whytecliff Park in southeastern Howe Sound. From the Upper Levels Highway, take Exit #1 for 400 metres and turn left onto the highway overpass. The overpass turns into Marine Drive. Follow Marine as it winds its way to Whytecliff Park. A large wooden sign marks the park. Park in the large parking lot. Either gear up here or carry your gear down the ramp and then left down the stairs to the beach. Whyte Islet is the large islet on the southern side of the bay. Take care negotiating the logs and rocks on the beach.

Hazards   Boat traffic, current, and fishing line (see page 12)

Description   Whyte Islet is a very popular dive site. On weekends, dive classes of all levels take place near the Islet, especially on its northern side. Most classes venture only to the mid point of the Islet, so divers seeking a less crowded, clearer dive should start about halfway out towards the west side or at the western tip. On weekdays, the crowds are usually gone, and the entire site is available for underwater touring.

The northern section of the islet is a rapidly descending series of rocky ledges. Depths in this part plummet past 100 feet very quickly. Walls and ledges, some of which have old cable, rope, tires, and cement blocks left over from the days when there was a marina at this site, are home to calcareous tube worms; sea stars; sea cucumbers; and white, lemon peel, and alabaster nudibranchs. White and orange plumose anemones are occasionally seen. Towards the western tip of the island, sloped sandy bottom replaces the ledges and meets the rock of the islet in 30 to 40 feet of water. Many brittle stars and large sea pens live in the sand. On the rocky islet, sunflower stars, yellow boring sponges, sea peaches, glassy sea squirts, and sea cucumbers can be found.

The western tip of the islet is a thin rocky point that spikes into the ocean to a depth of 90 feet. A beautiful large white plumose anemone field springs out of the rock. Beds of purple and green sea urchins abound. An octopus hides in a crevice. Colonies of zoanthids and giant barnacles cover several rocky outcroppings. Cloud sponges start in 70 feet. Lingcod and kelp greenlings hover in the area. Rounding the west tip and heading east along the south section of the islet, the bottom once more shallows to 40, then 20, then 10 feet. Kelp, barnacles, purple stars, blackeye gobies, and flatfish are common here.

Wheelchair access   Large logs, rocks, and a short steep slope to the beach make it difficult but not impossible to reach the water. Divers can be carried over these obstacles.

The islet at low tide

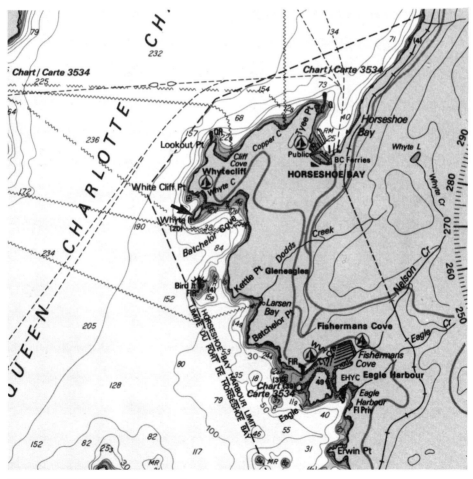

NOT TO BE USED FOR NAVIGATION—see page 9.
Use Canadian chart 3526 for navigation.
For information on obtaining navigational charts, see page 21.

87

132. Whytecliff Marker

Shore dive. . .intricate bottom with one of everything. . .variety of marine life, both vertebrate and invertebrate. . .a seal plays with divers. . .hazards are boat traffic, current, depth, and fishing line

Skill level   2 or 3 (see page 11)

Access   Shore dive

Location   Whytecliff Marker is on the northwest side of the bay at Whytecliff Park in southeastern Howe Sound. From the Upper Levels highway, take Exit #1 for 400 metres and turn left onto the overpass. The overpass turns into Marine Drive. Follow Marine as it twists and turns west to Whytecliff. The park is marked by a large wooden sign. Park in the large parking lot. Either gear up here or carry your gear down the ramp to the beach. On the northwest side of the bay is a circular tower with a green band on top. Snorkel to the tower or to the point at the north end of the bay, descend, and move west.

Hazards   Boat traffic, current, depth, and fishing line (see page 12)

Description   Whytecliff Marker warns boaters of a rocky reef hidden by high tides. It also marks one of the Vancouver area's most popular dive sites. A complex and lively bottom provides thousands of nooks and crannies to explore.

A labyrinth of paths twists through the reef's top 20 feet. Kelp and sea lettuce hang off some rocks. Huge schools of pile perch and shiner perch play in the shallow water. The southern section is a rounded wall that runs from 30 feet deep at the base of the eastern end to more than 100 feet to the west. A series of rock walls and sand and silt ledges makes up the western side of the reef. The ledges are home to two impressive white plumose anemone beds. Sea cucumbers, sunflower stars, rose stars, long ray stars, sea lemons, and white nudibranchs are also in the area. Deeper along this section are cloud sponges and lampshells. Lingcod and rockfish drift along the rock.

The northern section of the reef has very interesting geography. Sheer walls, ledges, small overhangs, and boulder-strewn areas allow for endless exploration. The marine life is also interesting. Zoanthids coat exposed boulders. Transparent and glassy sea squirts cling to other rocks. Snails and tritons move slowly along the bottom. Red Irish lords, copper and quillback rockfish, lingcod, and even dogfish are found. An octopus can be seen wedged in a crevice or sometimes out searching for food—bad news for the green and purple urchins and the red rock crabs on the reef. A friendly seal that lives in the Whytecliff area visits divers, especially on night dives, and has been known to swim within a few feet of pairs of dive buddies.

Wheelchair access   Access is the same as for Whyte Islet, or divers can be wheeled down the steps and carried over the logs for a shorter surface swim.

The white circular tower with green top band seen from the beach at Whytecliff Park

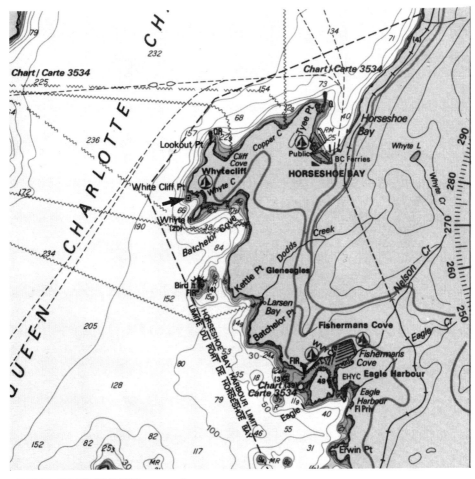

NOT TO BE USED FOR NAVIGATION—see page 9.
Use Canadian chart 3526 for navigation.
For information on obtaining navigational charts, see page 21.

89

133. The Cut North Wall

Shore dive. . .sheer wall drop past 100 feet. . .some ledges. . .good mix of marine life with man-made objects strewn about the ledges. . .hazards are boat traffic, depth, and fishing line

Skill level 3 (see page 11)

Access Shore dive

Location The Cut is located at the northern end of Whytecliff Park in southeastern Howe Sound. Take Exit #1 from the Upper Levels Highway. The first left takes you onto the highway overpass and then onto Marine Drive. Follow Marine as it twists and turns its way to Whytecliff Park. The park is marked by a large wooden sign. Once at Whytecliff, stay right and follow the road around the park and past the washrooms to the small lot near the sheltered lookout. A short winding trail south of the lookout leads to a miniature fjord known as the Cut. Enter the water here, swim to the north point, descend, and move north.

Hazards Boat traffic, depth, and fishing line (see page 12)

Description The Cut is a well-known site. Its name derives from the entry point's resemblance to a giant cut in the rocks of Whytecliff Park. Its popularity is based partly on the interesting marine life and partly on the man-made oddities strewn about the bottom. The north wall is a series of narrow sandy ledges that drop rapidly into very deep water. Trained divers who are able to venture to the limits of sport diving find large chimney and cloud sponges starting at 80 feet. Long ray stars, nicknamed Velcro stars because of the way they stick onto neoprene diving gloves, sprawl on the bottom. Large tiger prawns and very large lingcod also inhabit the deeper waters.

Shallower ledges yield a greater variety of colourful life as well as some man-made objects. Orange and white plumose anemones, calcareous tube worms, and thatched barnacles lie in groups. Sea cucumbers, sea firs, swimming scallops, purple urchins, gumboot chitons, stalked hairy sea squirts, and several different types of sea stars lie individually throughout the site. Galathaeid crabs and umbrella crabs move about the ledges. Hiding in a crevice is an octopus. Careful observation leads to sightings of red Irish lords and buffalo sculpins. The sandy sections of the ledges are home to sea pens and tube-dwelling anemones.

Human additions to the site include beer and pop bottles with sea squirts, limpets, and armoured sea cucumbers attached; running shoes; T-shirts; a road sign; and a construction warning barrier. Anything providing habitat should be left on the bottom.

Wheelchair access Access via the Cut is impassable to chairs. It is possible to enter through the bay at Whytecliff (see Whyte Islet, p. 86) and then swim around the point.

The entry

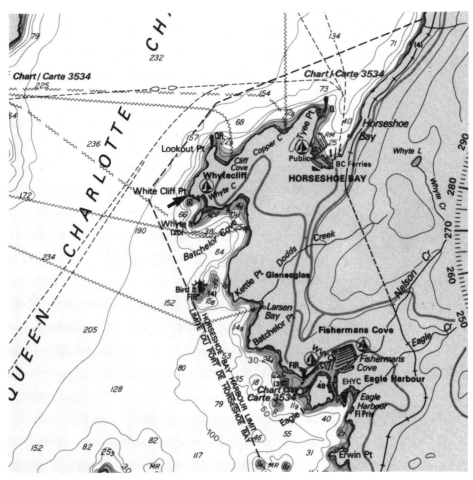

NOT TO BE USED FOR NAVIGATION—see page 9.
Use Canadian chart 3526 for navigation.
For information on obtaining navigational charts, see page 21.

91

134. Lookout Point

Shore dive. . .sand and shallow wall at beginning gives way to series of ledges that go as deep as divers' ability. . .life everywhere, including variety of fish and invertebrates . . .hazards are boat traffic and current

Skill level   2 or 3 (see page 11)

Access   Shore dive

Location   Lookout Point is between Whytecliff Park and Horseshoe Bay in southeastern Howe Sound. From the Upper Levels Highway, take Exit #1 for 400 metres and turn left. The left turn takes you over the highway and onto Marine Drive. Follow Marine past Whytecliff Park, where it becomes Arbutus Drive. A T-junction marks the intersection of Arbutus Drive and Arbutus Place. Park here off the road and follow the Beach Access sign down a short trail and a set of stairs to the beach. Lookout Point is on the northwest side of the bay, just past a ramshackle boathouse. Be careful when negotiating the rocky beach as it can be very slippery.

Hazards   Boat traffic and current at the point (see page 12)

Description   Lookout Point is one of the Greater Vancouver area's best shore dives. The rocky shore hides purple shore crabs, hairy shore crabs, small sea stars, and fish. Large brown kelp leaves and slippery green seaweed cling to the larger rocks in the lower intertidal zone. Divers can fin along the bottom or snorkel west until they meet the 15- to 20-foot vertical wall and then head north. The wall runs for several hundred feet and is home to purple stars, blackeye gobies, rockfish, lingcod, blood stars, and leather stars.

The beginning of the point is marked by a large crevice in the wall with a cement highway divider at its base. Large numbers of fish, including yelloweye rockfish, lingcod, quillback rockfish, canary rockfish, and striped perch, swim in and out of the crevice. From here the bottom drops away, and the direction of travel changes from north to west as you round the point. This is where the current is found. The wall becomes a series of ledges, each with its own particular grouping of life. One ledge hosts a forest of white plumose anemones. Another has zoanthid-coated boulders. Sea peaches, glassy sea squirts, calcareous tube worms, barnacles, and purple urchins all have their colonies. Divers also see painted stars, long ray stars, swimming scallops, whelks, snails, nudibranchs, and tealia anemones. Hairy lithode crabs, heart crabs, and octopuses can be spotted hiding in cracks and under rocks. Fish seem to follow divers everywhere. Grunt sculpins, red Irish lords, and a host of other fish allow divers close enough for a good look. Deeper sections of the point, 80 to 100 feet, have chimney and cloud sponges, some with galathaeid crabs or coonstripe shrimp nestled inside.

Wheelchair access   The stairs, logs, and rocks make this site hard for able-bodied divers to reach. Divers who use wheelchairs are advised to make this a boat dive. It is well worth the trip.

The ramshackle boathouse and the rocky point

NOT TO BE USED FOR NAVIGATION—see page 9.
Use Canadian chart 3526 for navigation.
For information on obtaining navigational charts, see page 21.

93

135. Cliff Cove East

Shore dive. . .simple wall, with depths to 40 feet. . .odd rocky outcropping. . .lots of life, especially fish and sea stars. . .hazard is boat traffic

Skill level   1 (see page 11)

Access   Shore dive

Location   Cliff Cove East is between Whytecliff Park and Horseshoe Bay in southeastern Howe Sound. From the Upper Levels Highway, take Exit #1 for 400 metres. Turn left and follow the overpass over the highway and onto Marine Drive. Follow Marine past Whytecliff Park, where it becomes Arbutus Drive. A T-junction marks the intersection of Arbutus Drive and Arbutus Place. Park here off the road and follow the Beach Access sign down a narrow trail and a set of wooden stairs to the beach. Cliff Cove East is on the eastern side of the bay. The rocks on the beach are sometimes slippery, so divers should be careful when heading to the water.

Hazards   Boat traffic (see page 12)

Description   Cliff Cove East is an easy dive with a shallow rock wall and a flat sandy bottom for divers to investigate. Depths never exceed 40 feet except at the northern section of the wall. An occasional rocky outcropping on the wall provides a playground for many types of fish and starfish. A large rockslide with rusty metal latticework sticking out of it marks the northern end of the dive. From here, the bottom slopes away quickly and the marine life becomes sparse.

Swimming north along the wall, divers see a host of purple stars clustered in the intertidal zone. Leather stars, rose stars, painted stars, and sunflower stars also dot the area. Some of the larger rocks are covered in orange zoanthid colonies. Yellow margin nudibranchs, orange finger sponge, velvety red sponges, swimming scallops, green sea urchins, and barnacles provide flashes of colour. Shrimp, hermit crabs, and red rock crabs move in all directions or sit motionless on the rocks observing other life.

The most impressive feature of Cliff Cove East is the variety of the fish seen here. Large lingcod and kelp greenlings abound. Hiding in and around the rocky outcropping along the wall are copper rockfish, quillback rockfish, tiger rockfish, canary rockfish, and yelloweye rockfish. Blackeye gobies lying out in the open dart into dens when divers swim past. A careful inspection of crevices can turn up a purple plainfin midshipman, also called a toadfish. Schooling fish such as shiner perch, striped perch, and tube snouts move in their groups around the base of the wall.

Divers with a bit of air left over can tour the gently sloped sand bottom of the bay. Flatfish, grunt sculpins, crabs, and man-made articles are all over the sand. They are worth a look, and, if you judge the distance correctly, you can end up at the shore at your exit point.

Wheelchair access   The wooden stairs and rocky beach make this a difficult site for wheelchair divers. It is probably best reached by boat.

The wall seen from across the beach

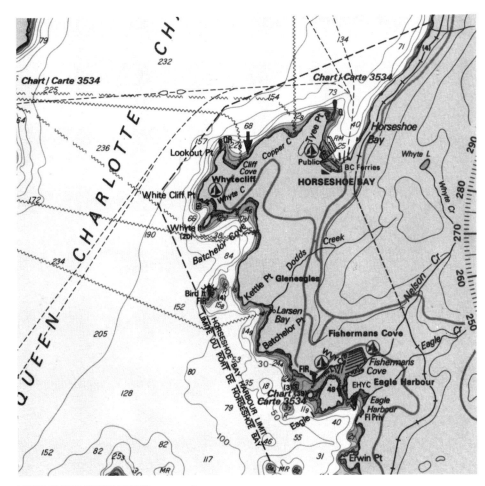

136. Copper Cove

Shore dive. . .shallow dive with rocky slope and sand slope. . .good variety of marine life. . .some bottles and other man-made objects. . .take care on rocks at entry. . .hazards are boat traffic and current

Skill level   1 (see page 11)

Access   Shore dive

Location   Copper Cove is between Whytecliff Park and Horseshoe Bay in southeastern Howe Sound. From the Upper Levels Highway, take Exit #1 for 400 metres and turn left onto the highway overpass. This leads onto Marine Drive. Follow Marine a short way and turn right onto Copper Cove Road. Drive to the turnaround at the end of Copper Cove Road, unload your gear, and park up the road. Gear up and walk down the set of wooden steps to the pilings, which are all that remains of a large dock. Enter here and move north. Be careful when walking on the slippery rocks at the entry to the dive.

Hazards   Boat traffic and current (see page 12)

Description   Copper Cove is a shallow wonderland great at night and during the day. A rocky foreshore descends into 15 feet of water before giving way to a gently sloped sand bottom. As you head north, the sand slope becomes a medium grade at the base of a steep rocky slope descending from the shore to 40 to 45 feet. It is possible to swim beyond the point and head west for a distance, encountering the same rock and sand slopes.

The shallow water near the entry is full of large rocks coated with barnacles, purple stars, sea lettuce, and rockweed. Small shore crabs run over and between the rocks. Clam and cockle shells and siphons litter the sloped sand. Short-spined stars, sea pens, sole, buried tealia anemones, and tube-dwelling anemones also inhabit the sand. Scuttling between the sand and rock are red rock crabs. Some bottles, tires, and old float lines are in the area.

Most of the marine life is found around the rocky sections adjacent to the shore. Bull kelp and broad leaf kelp that cling to the rock provide homes for nudibranchs and encrusting bryozoans. Orange, white, and grey plumose anemones guard the area. Also on the rocks are stalked hairy sea squirts, light bulb tunicates, sea peaches, sunflower stars, painted stars, false Pacific jingle shells, lined chitons, orange and California sea cucumbers, and nudibranchs. Giant barnacles covered in orange encrusting sponge are on the rocks near the point. Red Irish lords and buffalo sculpins lie well camouflaged. An octopus can be seen hiding in a crack. Copper rockfish and kelp greenlings swim lazily through the area.

Wheelchair access   Stairs and a rocky entry make this a difficult site to reach.

The remains of the dock, with the rocks of the western side of the cove in the background

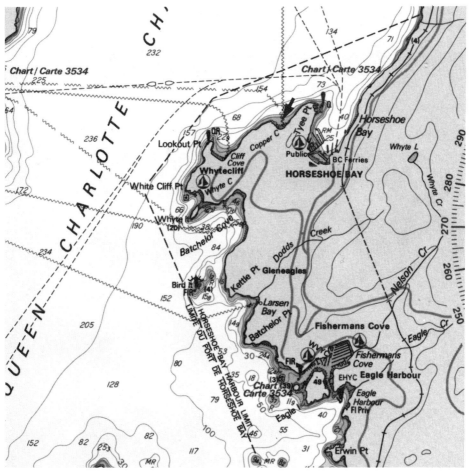

NOT TO BE USED FOR NAVIGATION—see page 9.
Use Canadian chart 3526 for navigation.
For information on obtaining navigational charts, see page 21.

97

137. Sunset Beach South

Boat dive. . .a series of small drops and a sand slope run to 100 feet or more within a compact area. . .vegetation in shallow water; fish and invertebrates in medium and deep water. . .hazards are boat traffic and current

Skill level   3 (see page 11)

Access   Boat dive

Location   Sunset Beach is 3.7 kilometres (2 nautical miles) north of Horseshoe Bay on the eastern shore of Howe Sound. The dive site is .9 kilometre (.5 nautical mile) south of the Sunset Marina along the face of the prominent wall. Look for the sign marking an outfall pipe that lies along the southern section of the site; the pipe should be avoided when anchoring. Anchorage in shallow water with good holding ground is available in a small bay in the southern section. Descend the anchor line and move north.

Hazards   Boat traffic and current (see page 12)

Description   The wall face south of Sunset Beach South is a compact dive with deep and shallow water attractions. It is an ideal dive for divers wishing to head out deep and come back shallow over a small area. A short drop from the surface to 15 to 25 feet is followed by a sloping sand section which runs to about 60 feet. From there a series of small walls and rocky outcroppings descends past 100 feet.

The shallows of Sunset Beach South are covered with algae, encrusting bryozoans, purple stars, sunflower stars, leather stars, and kelp. Green and red sea lettuce and rockweed also cling to the bottom. Kelp greenlings dart about the base of the shallow drop. Many empty clam shells lie littering the sloped area. Some siphons stick out of the sand.

In the mid-depth range are orange and California cucumbers, sea lemons, white and alabaster nudibranchs, yellow boring sponge, orange and grey mottled slime stars, lined chitons, painted brittle stars, and stalked hairy sea squirts.

In the deeper sections, calcareous tube worms, lampshells, crimson anemones, warty tunicates, slippered cucumbers, cloud sponges, and prawns can be found along the walls and outcroppings. Lingcod and black rockfish move slowly about the walls.

The waterfront at low tide, with a sign on the right warning of a submerged cable

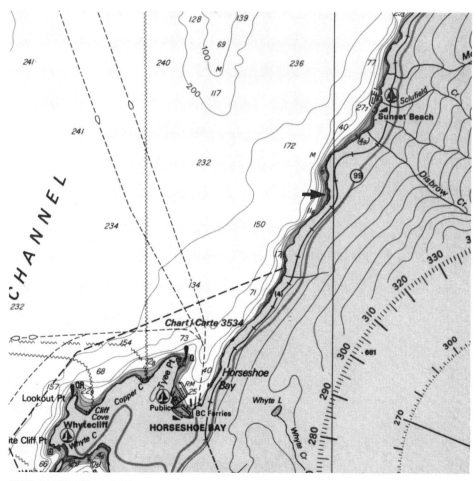

NOT TO BE USED FOR NAVIGATION—see page 9.
Use Canadian chart 3526 for navigation.
For information on obtaining navigational charts, see page 21.

99

138. Bowyer Island South

Boat dive. . .mixed bottom with wall south of island, sand slope east, and rocky medium slope west. . .wolf eels and octopus highlight marine life. . .hazards are boat traffic, current, and wind

Skill level   1, 2, or 3 (see page 11)

Access   Boat dive

Location   Bowyer Island is located 4.6 kilometres (2.5 nautical miles) north of Horseshoe Bay in southeastern Howe Sound. The dive site is on the south tip of the island. A square-shaped brown house can be used as a reference (see photo). Anchorage is available to the east of the south tip of the island in shallow sand bottom. Caution should be exercised, as this area is open to winds from the south that can make anchoring difficult. Descend the anchor line and move south and then west for a deep dive or east for a shallow dive.

Hazards   Boat traffic, current, and wind (see page 12)

Description   The south tip of Bowyer Island ranges from deep walls to shallow rock and has great marine life. The rock and sand slope of the shore descends at a medium grade into 35 to 40 feet of water. It then drops sharply and becomes a silty wall that reaches depths of over 100 feet directly south and east of the point. On the east side, a sand slope descends from the rocky grade at 30 feet. On the west side, the sand bottom is strewn with rocks and boulders.

The deep wall south of the point has interesting life associated with deep water: intricate cloud sponges, patches of calcareous tube worms, and rows of chimney sponges. Hiding in the sponges are tiny decorator crabs and small red shrimp. Sea firs, zoanthids, vermilion stars, rose stars and red sea urchins are in the deep and medium-depth water. In the medium depths, 40 to 80 feet, are white plumose anemones; swimming scallops; alabaster, white, and yellow margin nudibranchs; yellow boring sponge; gumboot chitons; warty tunicates; glassy sea squirts; painted stars; sunflower stars; red and grey brittle stars; and pink, red, and white blood stars. The sandy area to the east of the point has wolf eels, octopuses, sea pens, and sea whips. Divers can also see lingcod, kelp greenlings, red Irish lords, rockfish, and brotulas.

In shallow water around the base of the island, kelp, algae, sea lettuce, and rockweed blanket the rocks. Sea peaches, green sea urchins, leather stars, short-spined stars, purple stars, and California cucumbers move about the rocks and vegetation.

The south tip of the island seen from the south

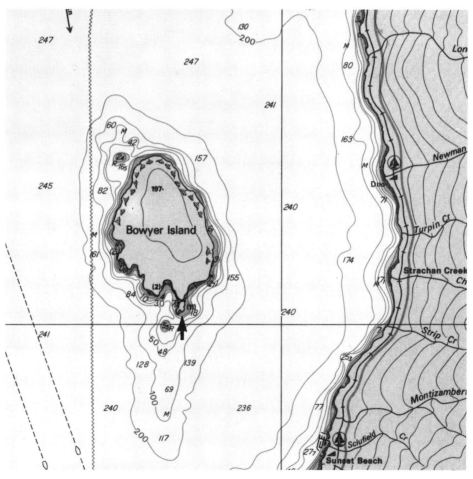

NOT TO BE USED FOR NAVIGATION—see page 9.
Use Canadian chart 3526 for navigation.
For information on obtaining navigational charts, see page 21.

101

139. Bowyer Island East Wall

Boat dive. . .sheer wall dropping out of sight to depths past 130 feet. . .beautiful cloud and chimney sponges, colourful marine life. . .hazards are boat traffic and depth

Skill level 4 (see page 11)

Access Boat dive

Location Bowyer Island is 4.6 kilometres (2.5 nautical miles) north of Horseshoe Bay in southeastern Howe Sound. The northeastern section of the island is mainly rugged cliff face with small indentations and one long thin bight. The dive site is along the cliff face north of the bight and is marked by a large boulder on its southern part and a 90-degree turn on its north (see photo). Anchorage is difficult for all but very small boats, so a tended boat is recommended. Descend on the inside of the 90-degree turn and move south.

Hazards Boat traffic and depth (see page 12)

Description Bowyer Island's east wall is one of Howe Sound's premier sponge dives. Definitely a dive for those with deep diving skills, this underwater section of Bowyer is a steep cliff of greater size than that above water. Even at 120 feet, it is impossible to see bottom.

Intricate and ornate cloud sponges start in 65 feet and continue down past sport diving limits. Their pale colour emerges out of the deep, dark water like radiant ghosts flashing to life at the touch of a light beam. They provide homes for green, red, and coonstripe shrimp; decorator and galathaeid crabs; and tiny rockfish. Forests of brooding silt-covered chimney sponges add their large tube-shaped bodies to the wall and also provide homes for other life.

Divers' eyes feast on multicoloured marine creatures. Slippered and California cucumbers, blood and vermilion stars, painted brittle stars, broad base sea squirts, and crimson anemones provide red colour on the wall. Orange is seen on sea pens, plumose anemones, encrusting sponge on giant barnacles, swimming anemones, and zoanthids. Yellow is seen on yellow boring sponge and cookie stars. White plumose anemones, limpets, and calcareous tube worms are also to be found. Near the northern end of the site, a large tree hangs upside down at about 70 feet, reaching into the deep water. On the surface, divers can spot several groups of seals lounging in the water or on rocks in the places where rocky foreshore breaks the uniformity of the cliff face.

The small sharp indentation at the north tip of the east wall

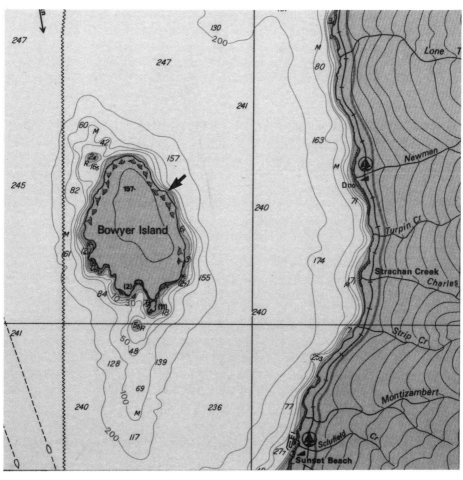

NOT TO BE USED FOR NAVIGATION—see page 9.
Use Canadian chart 3526 for navigation.
For information on obtaining navigational charts, see page 21.

103

140. Bowyer Island Pinnacle

Boat dive. . .rocky underwater pinnacle with one of just about everything. . .depths to 100 feet or more, but it is very easy to stay shallow. . .hazards are boat traffic and current

Skill level   1, 2, or 3 (see page 11)

Access   Boat dive

Location   Bowyer Island is 4.6 kilometres (2.5 nautical miles) north of Horseshoe Bay in southeastern Howe Sound. The dive site is on the northwest side of the island. To find it, look for the two large fissures in the rock of the island's northwest side. Between these fissures is a small point. Move west, 270 degrees true, from the point for approximately 200 metres. Watch your depth sounder, and drop anchor when the depth comes up to 20 to 40 feet. The pinnacle comes to 10 feet from the surface on very low tides, so vessels with deep draughts should take care when anchoring. This site is open to winds from the north, south, and west, so anchoring can be difficult.

Hazards   Boat traffic and current (see page 12)

Description   One of the best dives in Howe Sound. Bowyer Island Pinnacle has many types of sea creatures and an interesting bottom to explore. Divers of all levels find something to suit their tastes. The geography of the pinnacle is a mix of boulder-strewn flat sand and shell bottom, terraced rock, and sheer walls. Depths run to 100 feet or more, but it is very easy to find simple shallow areas to explore. There are many crevices and overhangs in the rock in both deep and shallow water.

The rocks and sand of Bowyer Pinnacle provide habitat for a great variety of marine life. Colonies of fluffy white plumose anemones, prickly green sea urchins, and bright orange zoanthids dot the rock. Heart crabs and Puget Sound king crabs lie motionless. Red rock, dungeness, and hermit crabs scuttle about the bottom. Yellow boring sponge, sea peaches, stalked hairy sea squirts, and wrinkled squirts adhere to overhangs or hide just on the edge of crevices. Deep inside crevices are octopuses and hairy lithode crabs. Red and purple urchins make their way slowly up and down the rocks. Divers interested in nudibranchs find many scattered throughout the site.

In the deep sections of the pinnacle live creamy white cloud sponges and silty grey chimney sponges. Brittle stars and long ray stars move across the deep sand. In the shallower sand, sea pens and tube-dwelling anemones gather. Scallop shells litter the sand areas. Surviving rock scallops and swimming scallops cling tenaciously to nearby rock.

Many fish live on the rocky pinnacle. Red Irish lords, buffalo sculpins, grunt sculpins, painted greenlings, kelp greenlings, and lingcod live on the nearby rock. Copper and quillback rockfish swim just above the pinnacle or wedge themselves into crevices. The fish have attracted the attention of some of the local seals. Divers can spot them on the surface before or after most dives and are sometimes lucky enough to be visited underwater.

The large crevices and logs that are the shore reference for the pinnacle

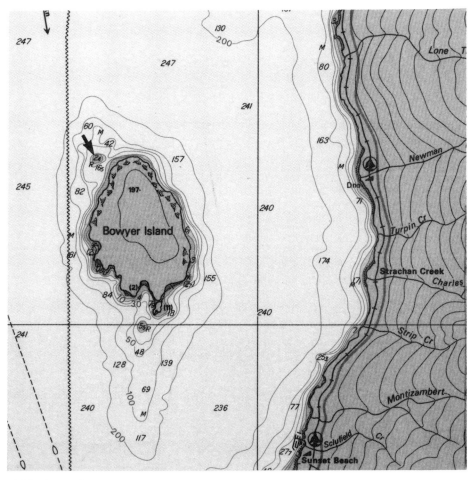

NOT TO BE USED FOR NAVIGATION—see page 9.
Use Canadian chart 3526 for navigation.
For information on obtaining navigational charts, see page 21.

105

141. Kelvin Grove South

Shore dive. . .easy wall. . .depths to 50 feet. . .sea stars, fish, sea squirts, octopuses
. . .hazard is poor visibility in summer

Skill level 1 (see page 11)

Access Shore dive

Location Kelvin Grove is in Lions Bay, 10 kilometres north of Horseshoe Bay on the
eastern shore of central Howe Sound. Take Highway 99 from Horseshoe Bay to Lions
Bay. The first exit at Lions Bay is Kelvin Grove Road. Turn left and left again at the T-junction.
Follow this road past the railroad tracks to a cul de sac. Unload your gear and park in
the lot just above the tracks. A dirt road leads past a set of wooden stairs and through
a small wooded area and ends at a sand beach. Washrooms are available during the
summer months in a small building on the west side of the path leading to the beach.
The west side of the rocky outcropping at the beach is the dive site. The hill between
the beach and the parking lot is long and steep, so be prepared to make a couple of
trips with your gear.

Hazards Poor visibility in summer (see page 12)

Description Kelvin Grove South is a simple, shallow, and super site. An easy entry,
a well-defined rock wall, and a vast array of sea creatures combine to make a great dive.
Depths at the base of the wall vary from 15 feet at the north end to 50 feet at the south
end. The south end of the wall is marked by a group of large rocks that gives way to
a medium-sloped sand bottom littered with clam and mussel shells.

The most noticeable inhabitants of Kelvin Grove South are sea stars; huge sunflower
stars and pink short-spined stars are immediately visible on the wall and in the sand at
its base. A rare northern sunstar, blood stars, leather stars, slime stars, and purple stars
also dot the site. Sea peaches, cup corals, plumose anemones, and orange and California
cucumbers all add colour to the area. Many cracks and crevices provide habitat for
vertebrates and invertebrates. Copper and quillback rockfish, plainfin midshipmen
(toadfish), and scaleyhead sculpins are found. Painted greenlings, kelp greenlings, and
lingcod also cruise through. Finding an octopus—always a highlight—is easy, as two have
taken up residence. Umbrella crabs, red sponges, and brittle stars also inhabit the wall.

Divers looking for more life can try the sand slope north of the wall. All types of sole,
clams, and anemones lie hidden or are partially buried in the sand.

Wheelchair access The south rock has two main obstacles for chairs. The first is the
steep hill leading down to the beach. Two able-bodied assistants should be able to
overcome this problem. The second obstacle, the sand slope and beach, can be
negotiated easily by the disabled diver, provided he or she is not dragging gear.

The rock and sand seen looking south from the top of the hill

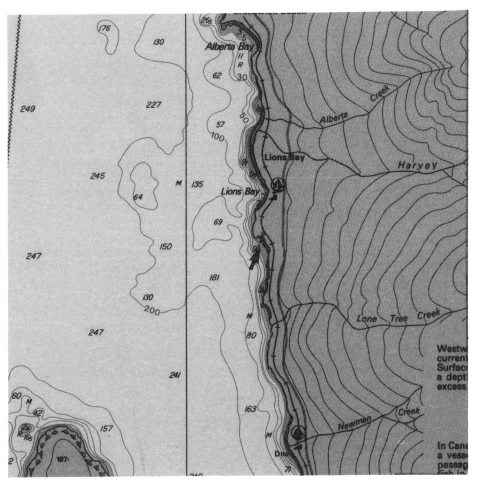

NOT TO BE USED FOR NAVIGATION—see page 9.
Use Canadian chart 3526 for navigation.
For information on obtaining navigational charts, see page 21.

107

142. Kelvin Grove North Wall

Shore dive. . .sand slopes, boulders, walls, overhangs, crevices. . .fish and invertebrates plentiful. . .hazards are boat traffic, current, and depth

Skill level   2 or 3 (see page 11)

Access   Shore dive

Location   Kelvin Grove is located in Lions Bay, 10 kilometres north of Horseshoe Bay on the eastern shore of central Howe Sound. Take Highway 99 from Horseshoe Bay to Lions Bay. The first exit at Lions Bay is Kelvin Grove Road. Turn left and left again at the T-junction. Follow this road past the railroad tracks to a cul de sac. Unload your gear and park in the lot just above the tracks. A dirt road leads to a set of wooden steps down to the beach. Washrooms on the west side on the dirt path leading to the beach are open during the summer months. Snorkel from the beach to the point on the north side of the bay. Descend at the point and move north. Kelvin Grove is known for the hill that divers must climb to get back to their cars. Be prepared for a couple of trips with your gear.

Hazards   Boat traffic, current, and depth (see page 12)

Description   Kelvin Grove Wall is one of the best shore dives in Howe Sound. Stunning geography and plentiful marine life are here, just a short drive from the city.

Boulder-strewn sand makes up the first section of the dive. This gradual slope runs several hundred feet west before giving way to a silt-covered rock drop-off. Giant nudibranchs, gobies, pink short-spined stars, and sunflower stars are in the sand or under the rocks.

About 30 metres north, the sand gives way to the first in a series of straight clifflike drops. Large cracks and crevices, a small cavern and a couple of impressive overhangs make the geography every bit as breathtaking as the variety of the marine life. Small silt-covered ledges pop out occasionally, but the drop runs past 100 feet very quickly. The northern end of the cliffs is marked by a sloped gravel bottom. Past 65 feet the cliffs are coated in calcareous tube worms, dotted with cloud and chimney sponges, and thick with shrimp and prawns. Between 20 and 60 feet the craggy rock is home to rockfish, shiner perch, lingcod, painted greenlings, and kelp greenlings. One huge zoanthid colony has its own wall. Orange and white cucumbers wave tentacles in the water in search of food. Dotting the wall are red and green urchins, slippered cucumbers, California cucumbers, yellow boring sponge, warty tunicates, sea peaches, lined chitons, decorator crabs, vermilion stars, slime stars, and umbrella crabs. In the shallow water, small crabs, kelp-encrusting bryozoans, and clam shells hide in the leafy kelp.

Wheelchair access   This site is best reached by boat or by using the entry to Kelvin Grove South Reef and swimming across the bay to the north point. See page 106.

The south tip seen from the west across the top of the access stairs

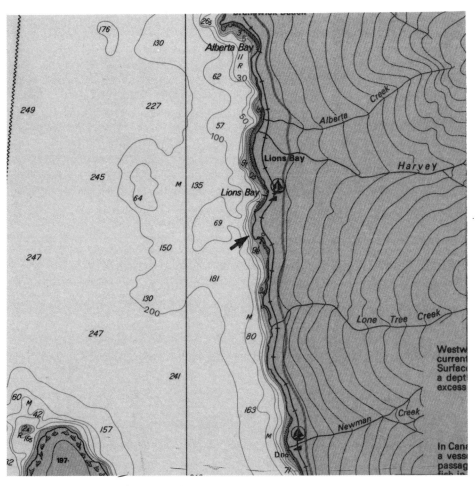

NOT TO BE USED FOR NAVIGATION—see page 9.
Use Canadian chart 3526 for navigation.
For information on obtaining navigational charts, see page 21.

109

143. Lions Bay Marina

Shore dive. . .winter only. . .rocky breakwater in marina, depths past 100 feet along rocks, steep sand north of breakwater. . .easy entry with fair marine life. . .hazards are boat traffic and fishing line

Skill level 2 or 3 (see page 11)

Access Shore dive

Location Lions Bay is 10 kilometres north of Horseshoe Bay on the eastern shore of central Howe Sound. Take Highway 99 north from Horseshoe Bay. At Lions Bay, follow the signs to the marina and park in the dirt parking lot. The dive site is the stone breakwater west of the boat ramp.

Hazards Boat traffic and fishing line (see page 12)

Description Easy entry and a short swim make the Lions Bay marina a prized shore dive. The marina is closed to divers during the summer months, when boat traffic is at its heaviest. During winter months, the marina is open only some days of the week, so it is best to phone ahead. The parking fee is ridiculously expensive, but, for groups that require immediate access to very deep water, the cost may be worth it.

The site drops immediately into very deep water and bottoms out at 100 feet at the base of the large rocks and boulders that were dumped to form the breakwater. Divers can explore deep or shallow along the tumbled rocks of the south and west sides of the breakwater and move beyond it to steeply sloped sand bottom on the north side. At the base of the western end of the rocks, a medium-sloped sand bottom may be beyond the limits of recreational diving, depending on height of tide.

The marine life at the Lions Bay Marina is not packed onto the rocks, but, since the site is so compact, divers do not have to move very far to find one of almost everything. On a dive here, you see lingcod, tiger rockfish, copper rockfish, painted greenlings, kelp greenlings, tube snouts, striped perch, and shiner perch. A small octopus may be seen somewhere in the rocks. Sea firs, sea peaches, stalked hairy sea squirts, calcareous tube worms, and cloud sponges are found at various depths. Swimming anemones and white plumose anemones live on the tops of rocks. Leather stars, sunflower stars, short-spined stars, and California cucumbers are draped over the breakwater.

On the deep sloped bottom west of the breakwater are man-made objects including tires, rope, wire, and cement blocks. A small work boat that has been weighed down with rocks to keep it on the bottom lies in 110 feet of water.

Wheelchair access Lions Bay Marina is an excellent dive for divers who use wheel-chairs. From the car to the water is a short trip, and the boat ramp provides an easy entry.

The access ramp and the stone breakwater of the marina

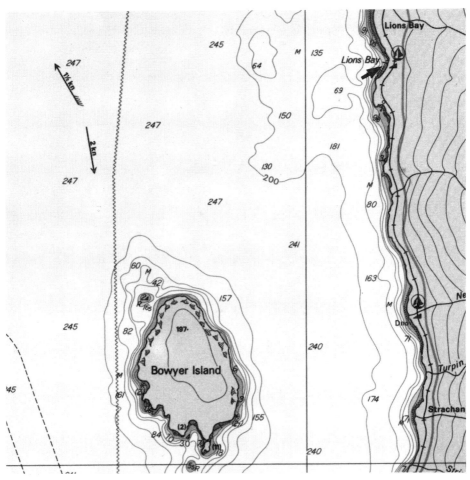

NOT TO BE USED FOR NAVIGATION—see page 9.
Use Canadian chart 3526 for navigation.
For information on obtaining navigational charts, see page 21.

111

144. M Creek North

Boat dive. . .deep wall plunging to 130 feet with a steep sand base and one steep sand drop on the wall itself. . .sponges and other deep life. . .good shallow life for multilevel or safety stops. . .hazard is depth

Skill level   3 (see page 11)

Access   Boat dive

Location   M Creek North is 12.2 kilometres (6.7 nautical miles) north of Horseshoe Bay on the eastern shore of Howe Sound. The dive site is the prominent point at the north end of the unnamed bay into which M Creek empties. Anchorage is difficult because of the steep bottom. A small bay east of the point can provide temporary anchorage when winds are calm. Enter north of the point and move south and then east around the tip, or enter on the east side and move west and then north.

Hazards   Depth (see page 12)

Description   M Creek North is a site for deep diving enthusiasts. Sheer cliffs plummet 120 to 130 feet before touching a steep sand and silt bottom on the southern and western sections of the dive. A sandy slope, running at such an incline you cannot help wondering how it stays in place, divides the rock face on the south side, providing some variety in the geography and marine life. This is an excellent site for multilevel dives, since deep water is easily accessible and all levels of the site host marine life.

   All the attractions of a deep dive are found at M Creek North. Beautiful cloud sponges shine yellowy white in the nearly dark world. Bright red galathaeid crabs, clown shrimp, coonstripe shrimp, and tiny copper and quillback rockfish hide in the cloud sponges and also in long silt-covered chimney sponges. Slippered cucumbers add their red, waving tentacles to the scene. Calcareous tube worms in white tubes extend coloured fanlike tentacles that swiftly retract when the water about them is disturbed.

   Large overhangs and deep fissures in the rock make for splendid viewing and exploration. In one section just north of the point, an awesome flat wall resembling the side of a building rises from the bottom. Colonies of zoanthids, glassy sea squirts, and slippered cucumbers hang from the wall. The sand slope is home to huge tube-dwelling anemones, legions of brittle stars, and large dendronotus rufus nudibranchs. The shallow sections of the M Creek site are covered in large kelp leaves. Kelp greenlings and many sculpins dart about the rocky slope.

The point seen from the south

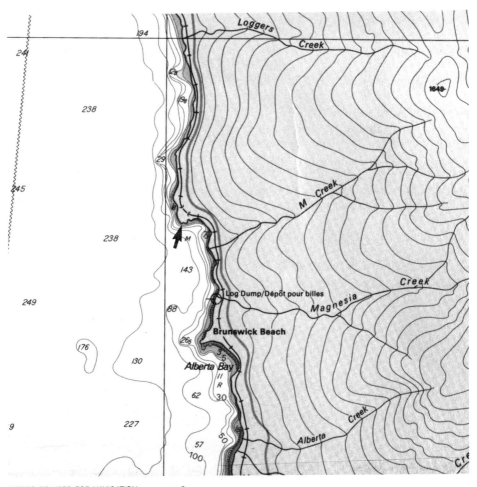

NOT TO BE USED FOR NAVIGATION—see page 9.
Use Canadian chart 3526 for navigation.
For information on obtaining navigational charts, see page 21.

113

145. Brunswick Point

Boat dive. . .wall with depths past 100 feet . . . marine life at all levels, highlighted by large orange finger sponges, octopus, buffalo sculpins, painted greenlings. . . hazards are depth and current

Skill level 2 or 3 (see page 11)

Access Boat dive

Location Brunswick Point is 3.7 kilometres (2 nautical miles) south of Porteau Cove on the eastern shore of Howe Sound. It is marked by a white circular tower with a red band on top and a red light that flashes after dusk. Anchorage is impossible at the point. A live boat is recommended in order to avoid the long swim to and from anchorage spots to the north and south.

Hazards Depth and current (see page 12)

Description As you may guess from the sight of the cliffs above water, Brunswick Point is a sheer wall dive. Depths can exceed 100 feet very close to the shore. A tiny ledge appears once in a while. Many cracks, crevices, and overhangs provide divers with ample territory for exploration. Some large rocks, the result of slides, lie in shallow areas, providing habitat for marine life. This is a good spot for multilevel dives.

Brunswick Point allows divers to go deep to see intricate cloud sponges, calcareous tube worms, long ray stars, and slippered cucumbers and then move into shallow water to explore cracks and crevices for other life. In the middle depths, between 40 and 80 feet, two huge zoanthid colonies coat the wall and orange encrusting sponges cover barnacles. Red and purple urchins, yellow boring sponge, swimming scallops, and an octopus are also at this level. White plumose, orange plumose, and crimson anemones appear sporadically.

In the shallowest water lies some of the most interesting life. The highlight of the dive is the large orange finger sponge growths, some of which measure almost two feet across and contain many branching fingers. There are also sea peaches, green urchins, sunflower stars, painted stars, sea lemons, California cucumbers, and orange sea cucumbers. Various fish swim close to the rocks. Painted greenlings (convict fish), lingcod, kelp greenlings, and buffalo sculpins can all be found resting on the bottom. Schooling in mid-water are pile perch and striped perch.

The white tower with red top band seen from the south

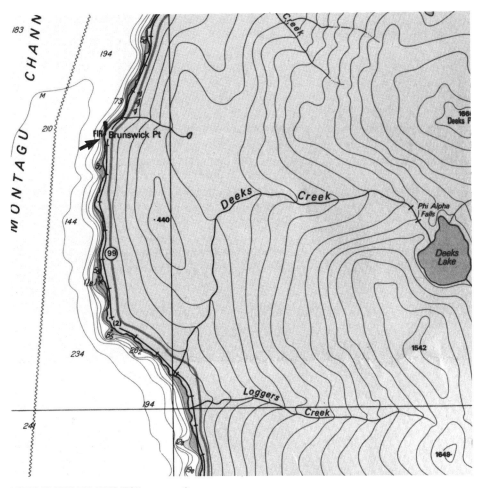

146. Porteau Wall

Shore dive...wall dive reaching 90 feet, with some ledges and interesting rock formations...unusual marine life including octopus, grunt sculpins, and hairy lithode and galathaeid crabs...hazards are depth and visibility

Skill level 2 or 3 (see page 11)

Access Shore dive

Location Porteau Wall is in the southern part of Porteau Cove Provincial Park in northeastern Howe Sound. Take Highway 99 north from Horseshoe Bay, turn left at Porteau Cove Provincial Park, cross the railroad tracks, and follow the road past the lower parking lot into the campground section. Drive through to the walk-in camping area, and park in the small parking lot. A narrow road, barricaded against cars, leads through the walk-in camps to the water via a small gravel beach on the west side of the road. Enter here, descend, and move south.

Hazards Depth and visibility (see page 12)

Description Porteau Wall starts out as a very shallow dive, 6 to 10 feet deep, with a gravel bottom inhabited by some clams, small crabs, purple stars, and sand dabs. As you move south, there is a dramatic drop. A series of straight drops and silt-covered ledges leads down to a base 90 feet deep. The wall is oriented north/south with a small east/west leg at the southern tip. Depths at the east/west section are 20 to 50 feet over some very interesting rock formations. At the base of the wall on all sections is a steep sand/silt slope.

Divers flock to Porteau Cove for the man-made underwater sights. At Porteau Wall, nature provides the scenery with some accidental assistance from humans. On the wall are zoanthids; coralene algae; cup corals; white and orange plumose anemones; encrusting bryozoans; warty tunicates; orange, California, and slippered cucumbers; glassy sea squirts; sunflower and brittle stars; shrimp; lampshells; swimming scallops; decorator, red rock, and galathaeid crabs; and an octopus.

The southern tip of the wall is a resting place for many pieces of old metal, including a large twisted sheet inhabited by calcareous tube worms, hairy lithode crabs, decorator crabs, chitons, scaleyhead sculpins, and coonstripe shrimp. In shallow water at 10 to 25 feet, sea peaches, mussels, barnacles, and ochre stars grow in abundance. Grunt sculpins, lingcod, and schools of striped perch are also found.

Wheelchair access A very good site for chairs. Divers can wheel to within a few feet of the water. Logs on the beach are more of an annoyance than a hazard.

Note: The campground is in use during summer months. A parking fee may be levied or access may be denied to divers.

The beach access to the site

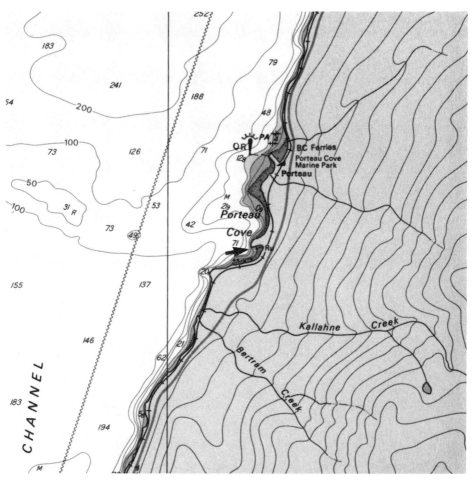

NOT TO BE USED FOR NAVIGATION—see page 9.
Use Canadian chart 3526 for navigation.
For information on obtaining navigational charts, see page 21.

117

147. Porteau Cove—The Bay

Shore dive. . .excellent onshore facilities. . .artificial reefs. . .marine life coming to live on the reefs. . .depths to 45 feet. . .hazards are wrecks, current, and wind

Skill level   1 (see page 11)

Access   Shore dive

Location   Porteau Cove is 10 kilometres north of Lions Bay on the eastern shore of Howe Sound. Take Highway 99, the Sea to Sky Highway, north from Horseshoe Bay. Ten kilometres past Lions Bay, look for a white and blue sign directing you to Porteau Cove Provincial Park. Turn left and park in the lower parking lot near the boat launch. Gear up and enter at the stairs on the north side of the parking lot.

Hazards   The wrecks, current, and wind (see page 12)

Description   During the 1980s and 1990s, tremendous effort was put into making Porteau Cove a divers' playground. Artificial reefs were sunk to attract marine life in an area out of bounds to boaters. Marker floats on the artificial reefs make them easy to find. There are indoor and outdoor showers, telephones, picnic tables, washrooms, a boat ramp, stairs down to the water, maps of the underwater attractions, marine life picture guides, facilities for windsurfers, and a ferry dock to combat highway closures due to rockslides.

The combination of facilities, easy-to-find underwater attractions, easy access, and shallow depths make Porteau a popular and fun spot to dive. White marker buoys that ring the site close it off to boaters. Two yellow floats mark the hull of a tug, the *Granthall*, and a rusty crane barge, the *Centennial III*. Near the barge lies a 40-foot ferrocement sailboat hull. The superstructures of the tug and the sailboat have been removed. Depths on the *Granthall* range from 15 feet at the bow to 45 feet at the stern. Divers can enter the cargo holds safely. The crane barge and sailboat hull are also in shallow water and can be carefully explored and passed through. The sailboat lies on its port side on quite an angle. In the area of the tug and crane barge is a jumbled pile of metal beams that divers can swim around and through. Orange and white plumose, shrimp, galathaeid crabs, grunt sculpins, kelp greenlings, lingcod, perch, and rockfish all move about the area.

A daisy chain of interlaced tires connects the wrecks with a collection of cement pilings, cement blocks, pontoon barges, storage containers, and slabs. This conglomeration is marked on the surface by a large wooden float. Fish, sea stars, nudibranchs, and an octopus all live in this section of the site. Depths range from 15 to 35 feet.

Wheelchair access   An excellent setup for disabled divers. Entry via the boat launch and a short swim to the marker floats make this site a natural.

The white markers prohibiting boats and the yellow markers and float marking dive attractions

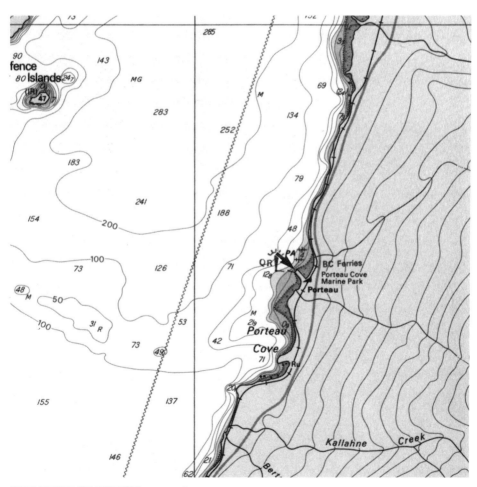

NOT TO BE USED FOR NAVIGATION—see page 9.
Use Canadian chart 3526 for navigation.
For information on obtaining navigational charts, see page 21.

119

148. Porteau Cove—The *Nakaya*

Shore dive. . .125-foot wreck of former minesweeper and fish packer, mainly intact. . . penetration not advised. . .some marine life. . .depths to 95 feet at low tides. . .hazards are the wreck, current, depth, and wind

Skill level   3 (see page 11)

Access   Shore dive

Location   The *Nakaya* is at the northern edge of Porteau Cove Provincial Park in northern Howe Sound. It is marked by a square wooden float with a wooden dive flag fixed to one corner. Divers can enter from the lower parking lot at the Provincial Park and snorkel about 200 metres to the wreck or park in the pullout on the east side of Highway 99 just north of the park, gear up, carefully cross the highway, climb very carefully down the steep rocky embankment, and then snorkel 25 metres to the wreck. Descend the float chain to 35 feet, where it branches off in three directions. Drop straight from this point for 20 to 25 feet and you are on the aft section of the wreck, or follow the thin yellow line from the chain to the aft section of the wheelhouse.

Hazards   The wreck, current, depth, and wind (see page 12)

Description   The *Nakaya* is a wooden 125-foot-long former minesweeper that saw service as a fish packer and a floating bunkhouse for tree planters. It was scuttled in 1985 as an artificial reef for divers. It lies on a north/south line slightly on the port side, with the bow in 95 feet and the stern in 50 feet at low tides. The hull is still intact, although sections of the starboard side and most of the stern decking are noticeably eaten away and decay is evident in other areas. The vessel is an eerie sight in the dark muddy world under the waves.

A tour of the *Nakaya* can be accomplished on one tank, although the depth makes it a quick tour. Some fittings remain on the upper deck, particularly on the bow section, and steering gear is visible through the decaying aft decking. The rudders are partly buried in the muddy bottom of the cove. On the port side aft is a small workstation, part of which has fallen into the mud off the port side. The bridge, accommodation spaces, work spaces, and breezeways remain intact, but penetration below decks is not advised because of instability caused by years underwater. With a powerful light, divers can see all spaces within the wreck from the outside. The *Nakaya* is dangerous to enter without proper training and equipment.

A small variety of marine life lives on the *Nakaya*. Calcareous tube worms coat the sides. Shrimp and galathaeid crabs hop about the decks. An occasional long ray star or plumose anemone can be spotted. Rockfish and lingcod drift lazily over the decks.

Wheelchair access   Access via the lower parking lot boat ramp is the route for disabled divers. The swim out and back can be a long one, but the dive is worth it.

The float that marks the Nakaya *as seen from the highway*

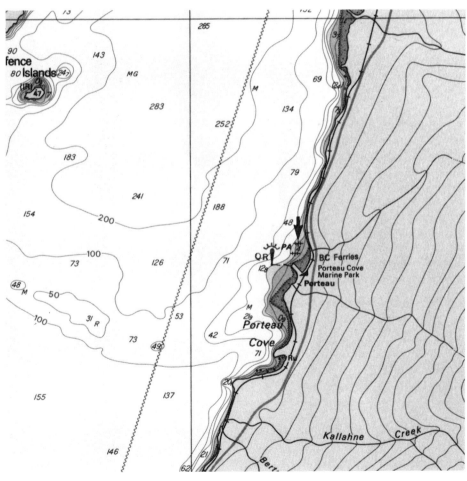

NOT TO BE USED FOR NAVIGATION—see page 9.
Use Canadian chart 3526 for navigation.
For information on obtaining navigational charts, see page 21.

121

149. North Porteau—Porteau Half Mile

Shore dive. . .a world of colour on a bleak mud background. . .medium slope to depths past 60 feet. . .best life is in shallow water. . .rocks and boulders provide habitat for many sea creatures. . .hazards are depth and visibility

Skill level   1 or 2 (see page 11)

Access   Shore dive

Location   North Porteau is located 1.8 kilometres north of Porteau Cove in northeastern Howe Sound. Take Highway 99 north from Horseshoe Bay and drive 1.8 kilometres past Porteau Cove Provincial Park. On the west side of the highway are two small gravel pullouts that accommodate six to eight cars each. Park in the northern (second) pullout. A narrow trail leads through the woods at a gentle slope to the railroad tracks. Cross the tracks, pick up the trail 5 metres south (left), and follow it down to the water. Enter at the north edge of the rocks, descend, and move south. Exercise care when walking on the rocks around the entry, as they are slippery with water and algae.

Hazards   Depth and visibility (see page 12)

Description   North Porteau is an eerie site, where the colours of the marine life burst forth in contrast to the grey mud and silt bottom. The site is easy to explore. The bottom moves west at a medium slope. Rock and boulder outcroppings provide homes for the marine life. Most life is in 60 feet or shallower.

At first, North Porteau seems to be a bleak grey world with only a few clam siphons in residence. Then the rocks and boulders appear, and shining white and orange plumose anemones jump out of the gloom. Swimming anemones also dot the rocks. Thousands of coonstripe shrimp crowd the bottom. Lingcod, quillback rockfish, and scaleyhead sculpins engage in staring contests at close range. Dogfish and blackeye gobies observe divers for a short period and then dart away.

Close examination of the rocks reveals a good variety of life. Umbrella crabs, slippered cucumbers, California cucumbers, yellow margin nudibranchs, coralene algae, orange encrusting sponge, glassy sea squirts, and yellow margin nudibranchs lie scattered over the area. There are also white nudibranchs, purple stars, and ochre stars. Kelp leaves lie covered in encrusting bryozoans. Hermit, dungeness, and red rock crabs can be found burrowing in the mud or scurrying along the rocks.

Wheelchair access   The narrow wooded paths make this site impassable to all but the most determined of divers who use wheelchairs and their able-bodied assistants.

The sloping rocks that mark the beginning of the dive

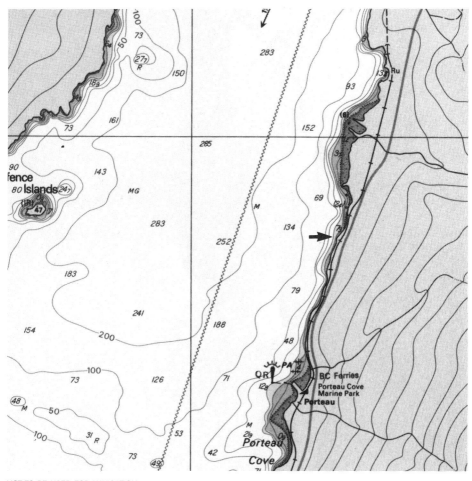

150. East Defence Island

Boat dive. . .medium to steep-sloped bottom. . .broken rock at shallow depths; silt, deeper. . .anemones of several varieties, shellfish, fish including dogfish, sea whips. . . hazards are wind and boat traffic

Skill level   1 or 2 (see page 11)

Access   Boat dive

Location   The Defence Islands are 3.3 kilometres (1.8 nautical miles) northwest of Porteau Cove in northern Howe Sound. Dive along the east side of the eastern island. The northeast side of the eastern island provides anchorage in shallow water with good holding ground. A rocky reef on the extreme northeastern tip is awash at low tides and should be avoided when anchoring. Gear up, enter the water, and move south.

Hazards   Wind and boat traffic (see page 12)

Description   East Defence Island looks like an anemone garden planted underwater. The rocky foreshore of the island descends as a mass of tumbled grey rocks to 15 to 25 feet before giving way to a medium-sloped silt bottom in the northern section and a steeper slope with some small wall faces in the south. Most of the marine life is in the top 60 feet.

Orange, grey, and white plumose anemones jump out of the grey silty background as soon as you descend on East Defence Island. They are a metre tall in some places. Tube-dwelling and slime feather dusters appear on the silt bottom. Swimming anemones and crimson anemones glue themselves to rocks scattered in the silt. Cup corals and zoanthids grow in loose colonies at most depths. The deeper waters are also home to lampshells; cloud sponges (growing in the silt!); terebellid worms; and long, slender sea whips that can reach a metre in height.

The medium and shallow water, 40 feet or less, holds the same plumose garden as the deeper water and also plays host to a variety of other life. Whelks and tritons live in large groups near the surface. Chitons, keyhole limpets, green urchins, and false Pacific jingle shells are found a little deeper. In the medium depths are sea peaches; California, orange, and slippered cucumbers; sunflower, painted, blood, and brittle stars; and stalked hairy sea squirts. Darting about the bottom are coonstripe shrimp, galathaeid crabs, decorator crabs, and red rock crabs. Lingcod, quillback rockfish, kelp greenlings, gobies, and the occasional dogfish fin their way through the water.

The east side of the island

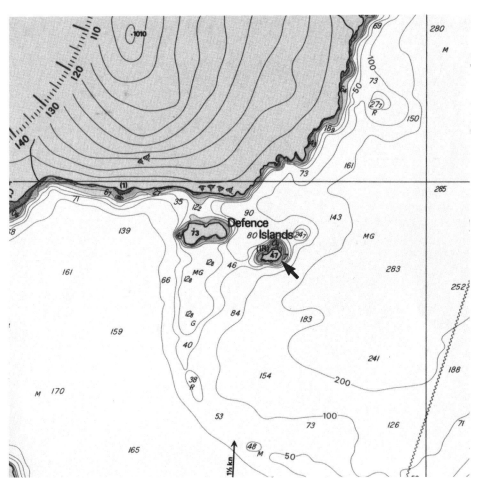

NOT TO BE USED FOR NAVIGATION—see page 9.
Use Canadian chart 3526 for navigation.
For information on obtaining navigational charts, see page 21.

125

151. West Defence Island

Boat dive. . .shallow plateau at western tip of island gives way to steep drop south and west. . .plumose, swimming anemones, urchins, and tritons are common in the shallow water. . .sea stars and tube worms are common deeper. . .dogfish in area can come close to divers. . .hazards are depth and boats

Skill level   3 (see page 11)

Access   Boat dive

Location   The Defence Islands are 3.3 kilometres (1.8 nautical miles) northwest of Porteau Cove in northern Howe Sound. The dive site is at the western tip of the west island. Anchorage is available close to the western tip of the island in fair holding ground. Care must be exercised when anchoring, as winds may cause anchors to drag.

Hazards   Depth and boats (see page 12)

Description   The most western of the two Defence Islands offers similar life to the eastern island but a very different geography. A shallow silty plateau averaging 25 to 35 feet in depth runs from the tip of the island. On the south and west sides of the plateau, a steep, silt-covered rocky drop-off gives divers the opportunity to experience the weightlessness of a wall dive. Depths here run past 100 feet. North of the plateau, shallow silty rock holds scarce marine life.

In the flat area of the plateau, divers find a large number of plumose anemones and sea peaches. Tritons, whelks, pink short-spined stars, green sea urchins, and dendronotus rufus are also visible. Tube-dwelling anemones wave arms, trapping and eating small shrimp that swim too close. Hovering in mid-water around the drop-off are long ray stars, tan cup corals, swimming anemones, slippered cucumbers, and lampshells. If you explore up and down, you find brittle stars, green sea urchins, calcareous tube worms, sunflower stars, rose stars, slime stars, painted stars, and glassy sea squirts. Painted tealias pop up occasionally. Barnacles coated in orange encrusting sponge lie glued to the rock. Dogfish up to three feet long may be encountered. They normally check out the new inhabitant of the underwater world soon after he or she has entered the water. Some dogfish are curious enough to come within one or two feet of a diver. Large lingcod, quillback rockfish, and the odd kelp greenling also swim about the area.

The west side of the island

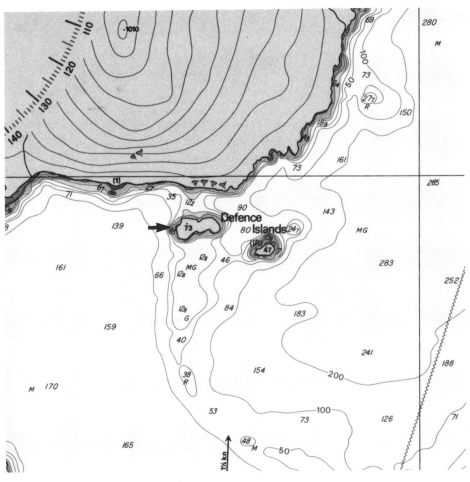

NOT TO BE USED FOR NAVIGATION—see page 9.
Use Canadian chart 3526 for navigation.
For information on obtaining navigational charts, see page 21.

127

152. Anvil Island West

Boat dive. . .wall with rounded rock, some tiny ledges. . .hundreds of dead cloud sponges in deep water. . .lots of life, including an octopus and an underwater spider. . .hazard is depth

Skill level   3 (see page 11)

Access   Boat dive

Location   Anvil Island is 4.3 kilometres (2.3 nautical miles) west of Porteau Cove in northern Howe Sound. The dive site is the western tip of the island, a prominent rocky point 2.5 kilometres (1.3 nautical miles) north of Irby Point. Anchorage is difficult, as there are only a few tiny ledges and a medium slope just south of the point on which to hang an anchor. A tended boat is advised.

Hazards   Depth (see page 12)

Description   Anvil Island West is a deep dive with a mystery. The depth can be 100 feet or more along the sheer wall. The only breaks in the drop are tiny silt-coated ledges and a small area just south of the point with a medium-sloped silt bottom peppered by a rockslide. Hundreds of dead cloud sponges' brown bodies adhere to the rock. The mystery is that they are dead although there is so much other life on the site.

Anvil West has a good sampling of living sea creatures for divers to observe. The deep waters are home to chimney sponges, calcareous tube worms, cookie stars, vermilion stars, lampshells, slippered cucumbers, crimson anemones, cup corals, and long ray stars. Shallower spots along the wall hold glassy sea squirts, stalked hairy sea squirts, warty tunicates, sea peaches, and zoanthids. Also found on the smooth, sculpted rock of the point are patches of yellow boring sponge and orange encrusting sponge; the latter grows in some places on giant barnacles. Painted stars, short-spined stars, and red and white blood stars dot the area. A ledge just south of the point is home to clumps of orange plumose anemones and beds of green sea urchins. One crevice in the wall holds a large octopus. Keyhole limpets are glued to the rock. Coonstripe shrimp bounce along the ledges, leaving wispy trails of displaced silt in their wake. A curiosity of the site during one of our dives was an underwater spider about the size and shape of a daddy-longlegs. It seemed quite comfortable strolling over the silt and rock but looked very much out of place.

The low rock that marks the dive on the west side of the island

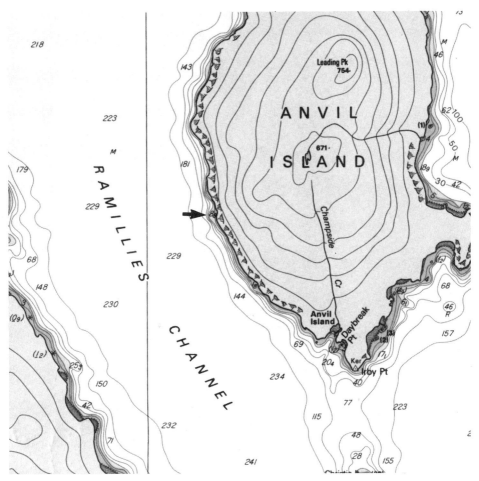

NOT TO BE USED FOR NAVIGATION—see page 9.
Use Canadian chart 3526 for navigation.
For information on obtaining navigational charts, see page 21.

129

153. Anvil Island Southeast

Boat dive. . .interesting geography includes peaks, valleys, overhangs, walls, and crevices. . .depth to 100 feet or more. . .many plumose beds and good mix of other life including octopus, dogfish, sponges, and sea stars. . .hazards are depth and current

Skill level   2 or 3 (see page 11)

Access   Boat dive

Location   Anvil Island is 4.3 kilometres (2.3 nautical miles) west of Porteau Cove in northern Howe Sound. The southeast section sticks out from the main body of the island as a hammer-shaped peninsula. The dive is along the southern tip of this peninsula. Anchorage is available near the southeast edge of the site in shallow water with good holding ground. Descend the anchor line and move west.

Hazards   Depth and current (see page 12)

Description   Interesting geography and bed after bed of plumose anemones are the main attractions at Anvil Island Southeast. A gently sloped silt, sand, and rock bottom descends from the edge of the island into 25 to 35 feet of water. Rolling rocky ridges that begin at this point provide peaks, valleys, overhangs, walls, and deep crevices to observe and explore. Depths reach over 100 feet along the southern sections. Each rocky area has its own group of orange and white plumose anemones numbering from 5 to 100 individuals of all sizes. The proliferation of these plantlike animals is quite lovely.

Anvil Island Southeast has a variety of attractions in addition to the geography and anemones. In the deep sections, cloud and chimney sponge formations hang from the rock. Orange and tan cup corals decorate other areas. Crimson anemones, swimming anemones, and zoanthids are found. Rose stars, slime stars, and painted stars are draped over some rocks. Adhered to others are lampshells, slippered cucumbers, swimming scallops, orange finger sponges, volcano barnacles, green sea urchins, and sea peaches. Prowling about the bottom are yellow margin nudibranchs, California cucumbers, galathaeid crabs, and shrimp. Hiding in a large crevice is an octopus. Swimming just off the bottom are lingcod, kelp greenlings, and the odd dogfish. The dive is especially fun if you manage to catch a nice, slow current ride back to the boat. Watching the varied bottom move by is a great feeling.

The southeast tip of the island seen from the south

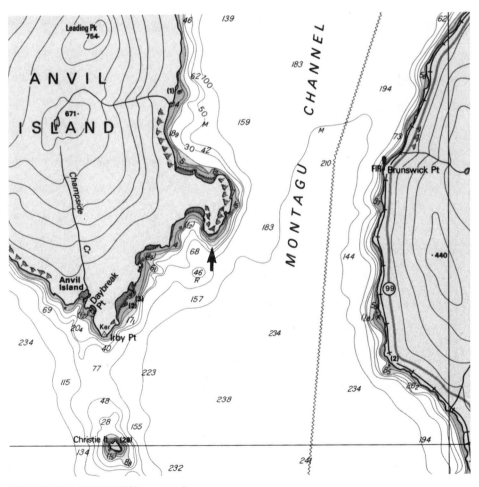

NOT TO BE USED FOR NAVIGATION—see page 9.
Use Canadian chart 3526 for navigation.
For information on obtaining navigational charts, see page 21.

131

154. Irby Point

Boat dive. . . medium to steep rocky grade with ledges in 40 to 55 feet. . . life at all depths and some interesting rock formations at 40 to 50 feet. . . hazard is depth

Skill level   2 or 3 (see page 11)

Access   Boat dive

Location   Irby Point is the southern tip of Anvil Island, which is 4.3 kilometres (2.3 nautical miles) west of Porteau Cove in northern Howe Sound. Anchorage is available immediately to the east or west of the point in shallow water.

Hazards   Depth (see page 12)

Description   Irby Point offers a controlled deep dive and interesting medium and shallow depths for groups of mixed abilities and for multilevel divers. A medium and at times steep rocky slope descends to 100 feet at the tip of the point, with boulder-strewn ledges between 40 and 55 feet and cascading rock piles 20 feet and shallower. Depths at the base of the east and west sides of the point are shallower than at the south tip, reaching only 40 to 50 feet. At the base of the rock, a medium-grade sand slope descends into very deep water.

Life in the deep sections of Irby Point is typical of much of the deep life in Howe Sound. Black and grey long ray stars sprawl on the bottom. Calcareous tube worms, cloud sponges, lampshells, and crimson anemones dot the rocky landscape. The sand slopes at the base of the rock are choked with tube-dwelling anemones and spotted with orange plumose anemones.

In medium depths, 40 to 80 feet, divers find blood stars, rose stars, vermilion stars, sea firs, plumose anemones, cup corals, chimney sponges, slippered cucumbers, orange cucumbers and green sea urchins. Shrimp dart everywhere along the bottom. A large octopus is curled up under a larger boulder. On the ledges live sea pens, tennis ball sponges, and sea lemons. Some interesting rock formations and crevices are frequented by copper and quillback rockfish, yellow eye rockfish, and kelp greenlings.

The shallowest section of Irby Point has rock piles to explore. Hundreds of shelled creatures, including tritons, whelks, and snails live here. Sunflower stars and leather stars also prowl the area.

The point seen from the south

NOT TO BE USED FOR NAVIGATION—see page 9.
Use Canadian chart 3526 for navigation.
For information on obtaining navigational charts, see page 21.

133

155. Christie Islet

Boat dive...sand/shell bottom with occasional boulders and rocks...depths to 65 feet...barnacles and small life crowd intertidal area; good mix of sand- and rock-dwelling life deeper...hazards are boats and wind

Skill level   1 (see page 11)

Access   Boat dive

Location   Christie Islet is 14 kilometres (7.5 nautical miles) north of Horseshoe Bay in central Howe Sound. Anchorage is available on all sides of the islet but should be chosen carefully with regard to weather and wave conditions. Descend the anchor line and circle the island or patch dive sections of it.

Hazards   Boat traffic and wind (see page 12)

Description   Christie Islet offers an easy dive in a picturesque spot. Hundreds of birds that live on the islet sanctuary provide divers with an interesting view above the water as well as below. On a sunny day, surrounded by the mountains and wildlife, the islet is one of the most relaxing sites in Howe Sound.

Most of the underwater life is in 60 feet or less. The rock of the islet gives way to a sand and crushed shell bottom. Depths vary from 25 to 65 feet. The southeast side is the shallowest and the north side the deepest. Boulder fields and small walls are sprinkled throughout.

The foreshore around the islet has colonies of acorn barnacles, mussels, and purple stars packed tightly together. Small sculpins dart in and out of the many crevices and cracks in the intertidal zone. Around the base of the islet, orange, white, and grey plumose anemones grow in great profusion as individuals, not in colonies. Red, purple, and green urchins cling to rocks and boulders. Sea pens, tube-dwelling anemones, red and grey brittle stars, and crimson anemones inhabit the sand and shell bottom. Thousands of large and small shrimp dart about the base of the islet or hide in cracks or under rocks. Orange and white cucumbers lie filter feeding between rocks. On the rocks live alabaster and yellow margin nudibranchs, leafy hornmouths, tritons, blue top snails, warty tunicates, stalked hairy sea squirts, orange finger sponge, yellow boring sponge, and swimming scallops. Painted tealia and burrowing anemones appear at random. Kelp greenlings, copper rockfish, painted greenlings, and gobies also live in the waters around Christie Islet.

The islet with Anvil Island in the background

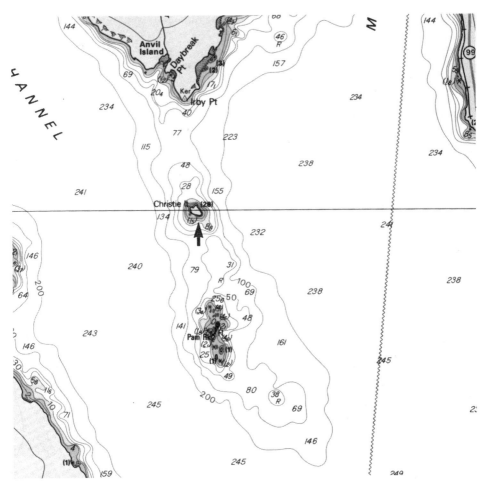

NOT TO BE USED FOR NAVIGATION—see page 9.
Use Canadian chart 3526 for navigation.
For information on obtaining navigational charts, see page 21.

135

156. Pam Rocks

Boat dive. . .seal dive, with very good mix of life in addition to the seals. . .varying geography. . .shallow, medium, and deep water. . .hazards are boat traffic and depth

Skill level 2 or 3 (see page 11)

Access Boat dive

Location Pam Rocks is a jumbled group of large and small rocks 12.2 kilometres (6.8 nautical miles) north of Horseshoe Bay in central Howe Sound. Anchorage is available to the east and west of the main rock, which is marked by a white circular tower on a cement base. Extreme care should be exercised when approaching and anchoring in this area, because many rocks are submerged or partly submerged at all times, especially to the north and south of the main rock. Once anchored, descend the line and move north.

Hazards Boat traffic and depth (see page 12)

Description Pam Rocks is the Vancouver area's best seal dive. The rotund little creatures are all over the rocks sunning themselves and staring wide-eyed at boats and divers. Some join divers underwater, swimming with amazing speed and grace despite their bulky appearance. Others approach within a few feet of divers on the surface, look them in the eye, submerge, and swim past under the surface. The frolicking seals and a great show of other marine life make Pam Rocks a prized diving site.

The bottom is a mix of gentle sand slopes, rocky outcroppings, ledges, and rock walls. Immediately east and west of the main rock, sandy slopes descend to 30 or 40 feet. North and south, shallow rocky outcroppings are common. Ledges and walls descend past 90 feet at the extreme east and west edges of the area.

The variety in bottom types allows for a wide selection of marine life. Sandy areas are crowded with tube-dwelling anemones, crabs, short-spined stars, and clams. Shallow rocky areas are covered in kelp, sea lettuce, mussels, tritons, leafy hornmouths, coralene algae, green urchins, and small sculpins. On the deeper ledges and walls are colonies of zoanthids, plumose anemones, and sea firs. Long ray stars, purple and red sea urchins, and white and orange sea cucumbers hide among scattered rocks. Galathaeid crabs stare out of cracks in the rock. Quillback and copper rockfish crowd into dens at all depths. Solitary lingcod and kelp greenlings slowly patrol the bottom or lie motionless, observing the other marine life. A spot fin sculpin can also be found.

The main rock and marker seen from the west

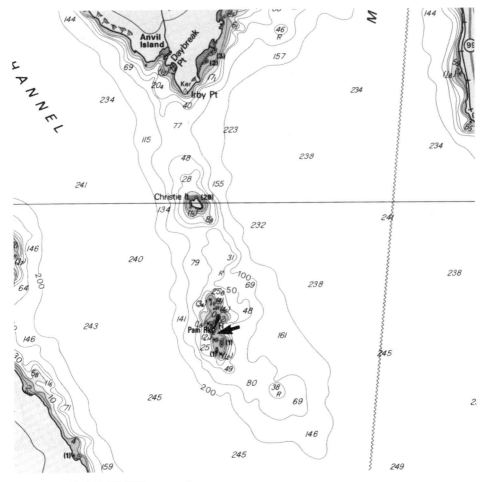

NOT TO BE USED FOR NAVIGATION—see page 9.
Use Canadian chart 3526 for navigation.
For information on obtaining navigational charts, see page 21.

137

157. Smugglers Cove

Shore dive. . .deep wall dive for newly experienced deep divers. . .shallow sand slopes at sides for other exploration. . .fair mix of marine life. . .hazard is depth

Skill level   2 or 3 (see page 11)

Access   Shore dive

Location   Smugglers Cove is on the north side of Bowen Island, 5.9 kilometres (3.2 nautical miles) northwest of Horseshoe Bay in central Howe Sound. From the ferry dock at Snug Cove, take Government Road and turn right onto Miller Road. Follow Miller past the United Church and turn left onto Hillcrest Road. Turn right onto Scarborough Road and then left on Eagle Cliff Road. Follow Eagle Cliff until it forks to the left as Hood Point Road. Drive along Hood Point Road and turn left on Finisterre Road and then left again onto Smugglers Cove Road. Turn right at the West Hood Point development and follow the paved road down to a cul de sac near the water. A short dirt road leads to the site.

Please note: Many roads on Bowen Island are not marked. There is a map on a large wooden sign on your right as you leave the ferry at Snug Cove.

Hazards   Depth (see page 12)

Description   Smugglers Cove is a good deep wall dive for those newly certified in deep diving. It also has shallow spots on either side that can be used for further exploration. The wall begins in about 30 feet of water directly north of a small rocky reef at the base of the roadway and drops past 100 feet.

Deep water attractions include chimney sponges, cloud sponges, calcareous tube worms, California cucumbers, sunflower stars, painted stars, slime stars, glassy sea squirts, Pacific pink scallops, and coonstripe shrimp.

In shallower water, down to 30 feet, a bottom of boulder, rock, sand, and shell provides habitat for sea life and areas for divers to explore. The rock and boulder sections are strung with broad kelp leaves, matted with orange encrusting sponge, and packed with purple sea stars. Yellow boring sponge, stalked hairy sea squirts, leather stars, and sunflower stars are here also. A sand slope to the west of the wall interrupts the rock bottom and makes a home for purple and pale-coloured tube-dwelling anemones and pink short-spined sea stars. Divers can find sailfin sculpins and buffalo sculpins at the site.

Wheelchair access   Excellent entry and exit for disabled divers. Cars can be brought close to the water.

The roadway and small rocky reef seen from the water

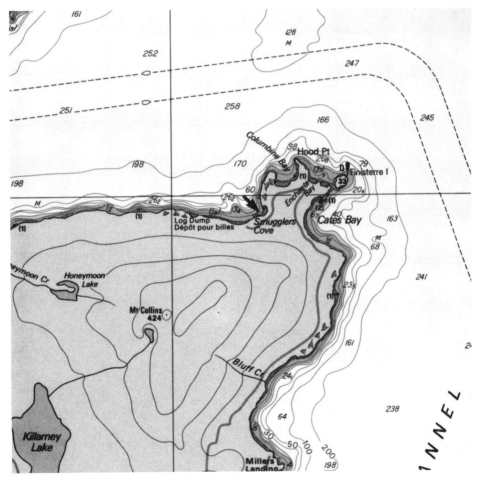

NOT TO BE USED FOR NAVIGATION—see page 9.
Use Canadian chart 3526 for navigation.
For information on obtaining navigational charts, see page 21.

139

158. Dorman Bay North Point

Boat dive. . .rocky wedge descends from shore to 90 feet. . .sand and rock around wedge attract lots of fish, octopus and sea stars. . .hazards are boat traffic, depth, and mild current

Skill level   2 or 3 (see page 11)

Access   Boat dive

Location   Dorman Bay is on the east side of Bowen Island just south of Snug Cove. A prominent rocky point marks the north tip of the bay. Anchorage south of the point is difficult, as the bottom slopes away quickly, but limited anchorage is available north of the point. A tended boat is recommended, especially on days with a north wind. Descend near the point and explore according to your level of training and experience.

Hazards   Boat traffic, depth, and mild current (see page 12)

Description   Dorman Bay's north point is a short boat ride from Snug Cove or Horseshoe Bay. Divers can go deep or shallow, depending on experience. The north point extends underwater as a rocky wedge driven into the sloping sand and shell bottom of eastern Bowen Island. The wedge reaches a maximum depth of 90 feet at its eastern tip and rises to the surface to meet the point at its north and south extremities. Some small boulders and rocks lying at the edges provide habitat for many creatures. Life can also be found in the sandy area around the rocks and on the rock wedge itself.

The shallow waters around Dorman Bay's north point are covered in kelp and surf grass. Mussels and purple stars cluster on the remaining exposed rock. Shore crabs scuttle about.

The sandy areas north and south of the rocky wedge are home to fields of sea pens, tube-dwelling anemones, and buried tealia anemones. Pink short-spined stars, blood stars, and sunflower stars dot the sand.

Small boulder and rock outcroppings provide habitat for zoanthids; glassy sea squirts; orange, white, and California sea cucumbers; yellow boring sponges; sea firs; and purple urchins. Two octopuses have dens in rock piles.

On the rocky wedge descending from the point are white and lemon peel nudibranchs, crimson anemones, rose stars, California sea cucumbers, heart crabs, and hairy lithode crabs. Various fish swim about the area. Schooling perch are seen throughout the shallow waters. Copper and tiger rockfish live in rock crevices. Large and small lingcod lie on the rocks. Spotting a ratfish or dogfish is also possible at this site.

The north point seen from the south

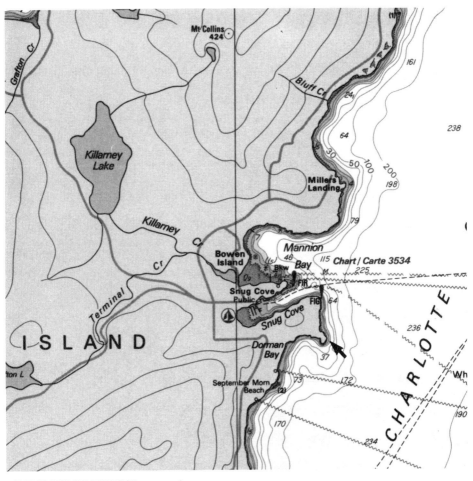

NOT TO BE USED FOR NAVIGATION—see page 9.
Use Canadian chart 3526 for navigation.
For information on obtaining navigational charts, see page 21.

141

159. Seymour Bay

Boat or shore dive. . .shallow wall and rock slope with sloping sand base. . .depths to 40 feet with north section sloping down to 100 or more. . .lots of fish and small invertebrates in vegetation. . .hazards are boat traffic, current, and depth

Skill level   1 or 3 (see page 11)

Access   Boat dive or shore dive

Location   Seymour Bay is near the southeast tip of Bowen Island, 7.4 kilometres (4 nautical miles) southwest of Horseshoe Bay in southeastern Howe Sound. Anchorage is available in the southern section of the bay, near a small islet that marks the dive site. Shore divers can reach the site by taking Government Road from the Snug Cove ferry terminal onto Grafton Road. Follow Grafton until it becomes Cowans Point Road and follow it to Seymour Bay. The road is very rough and hilly at some points and should be negotiated with care. The dive site begins at the base of the small islet on the southern tip of the bay.

Please note: Many roads on Bowen Island are not marked. There is a map on a large wooden sign on your right as you leave the ferry at Snug Cove.

Hazards   Boat traffic, current, and depth (see page 12)

Description   Seymour Bay appeals to divers who like to cover a small area and search meticulously for hidden treasures. There is much plant and animal life in mainly shallow water, and there is also a deep section for advanced divers. The rocky base of the islet is ringed by a forest of bull kelp and an undergrowth of broad leaf kelp, both sporting kelp-encrusting bryozoans. Depths run from 15 to 40 feet.

The intertidal area of the south and west sides of the islet is crammed full of mussels and barnacles filter feeding in the water. Large schools of shiner perch, pile perch, and striped seaperch swim in the shallow water. Gobies and small sculpins hide among the rocks and kelp. Purple and leather stars lie out in the open. Kelp greenlings make their solitary way through the bull kelp.

Below the bull kelp roots and to a depth of 40 feet, scattered rocks and a sloping sand bottom provide habitat for other creatures. Heart cockles, butter clams, and false Pacific jingle shells litter the bottom. Siphons from feeding clams stick out of the sand and withdraw quickly when touched. Vermilion stars, blood stars, sunflower stars, and pink short-spined stars pop up all around. Large gumboot chitons lie clinging to rocks. White, yellow margined, and Nanaimo nudibranchs are found on top of rocks. A pair of wolf eels is rumoured to be in the area.

To the north of the islet, a deep dimension is added to the dive. The sloping bottom is interrupted in several places by small ledges that shelter orange and white plumose anemones, lampshells, cloud sponges, sunflower stars, and large lingcod. Depths here run as deep as experience permits.

Wheelchair access   Difficult but not impossible as a shore dive. Fallen trees and driftwood are obstacles to the beach.

The small islet on the south side seen from the beach

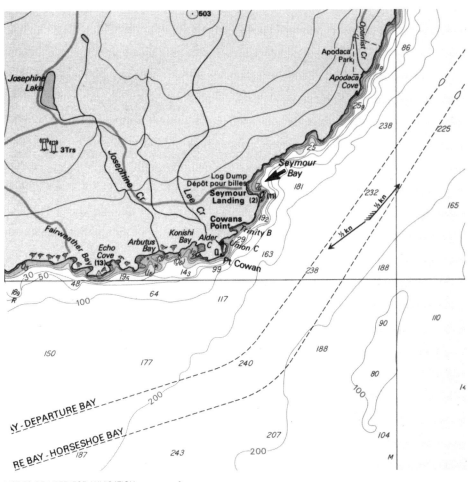

NOT TO BE USED FOR NAVIGATION—see page 9.
Use Canadian chart 3526 for navigation.
For information on obtaining navigational charts, see page 21.

143

160. Point Cowan

Boat dive. . .deep wall with intermittent shallow ledges and steep sand slope. . .depths past 100 feet. . .highlight is a large bed of crimson anemones. . .hazards are depth, boat traffic, and current

Skill level 3 (see page 11)

Access Boat dive

Location Point Cowan is on the southeast tip of Bowen Island, 8.3 kilometres (4.5 nautical miles) southwest of Horseshoe Bay in southern Howe Sound. It is marked by a white circular tower with a white light that flashes after dusk. Anchorage is not possible at Point Cowan, so a tended boat is recommended. Anchorage is available in Union Cove north of the marker for those who do not mind the swim. Enter either north of the marker at Union Cove or south of the marker.

Hazards Depth, boat traffic, and current (see page 12)

Description Point Cowan is a dive for those who enjoy going deep. A small ledge at 25 feet and other intermittent ones between 45 and 55 feet provide space for plant life and small marine creatures, but the majority of interesting life lies below 60 feet on a series of vertical drops and steep sandy slopes.

The shallow waters around the point are choked with bull kelp and broad leaf kelp. Pile perch and striped perch abound. Green sea urchins, purple stars, and the odd leather star lie exposed. Picking through the kelp, divers find blackeye gobies, northern ronquils, and scaleyhead sculpins mixed in with encrusting sponges and bryozoans.

The deeper waters, particularly those north of the marker, are home to large green painted tealias, huge cabezons, and big lingcod. A large rock wall 150 feet north of the marker provides the most interesting views. The wall starts in 50 feet of water and descends to 120 feet at its base. On top, white and orange plumose anemones wave tentacles in search of food. The face is dotted with plumose anemones, tealia anemones, tritons, hornmouths, striped sunstars, painted stars, and calcareous tube worms. The highlight of the wall is a dazzling patch of 80 to 100 crimson anemones. Other walls, which are smaller, have their own mix of creatures including blood stars, some white in colour; glassy sea squirts; opalescent and coryphella salmonacea nudibranchs; lined ribbon worms; and hermit crabs. Seams in the wall are home to rockfish.

The white circular tower with Union Cove on the right

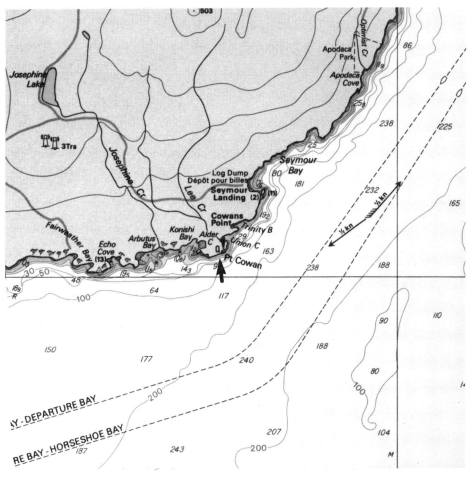

NOT TO BE USED FOR NAVIGATION—see page 9.
Use Canadian chart 3526 for navigation.
For information on obtaining navigational charts, see page 21.

145

161. Orr's Pinnacle (also called Hutt Island North Pinnacle)

Boat dive on rocky pinnacle with swim through hills and valleys. . .depths to 65 feet. . . good mix of marine life including anemones and fish. . . hazards are boat traffic and current

Skill level   2 (see page 11)

Access   Boat dive

Location   Orr's Pinnacle (it seemed like a good name to my friend Rob Orr) is 100 metres to the northwest of Hutt Island north marker, between Bowen and Hutt Islands in south central Howe Sound. The marker is a white and red triangular day marker on a wooden post atop a cement base. To find the dive site, travel northwest from the marker and watch for your depth sounder to read 15 to 20 feet. Anchorage is available in shallow water at the site in fair holding ground. Anchorage is difficult if a north or south wind is present. Descend and circle the pinnacle.

Hazards   Boat traffic and current (see page 12)

Description   Hutt Island Pinnacle is a rocky uprising covered in life. It reaches a maximum depth of 65 feet and always stays 15 to 20 feet under the surface. Rocks and rock walls that rise from a silt and sand bottom create a swim-through maze where divers can see everything from barnacles to zoanthids.

One circuit of the pinnacle can include sightings of brittle stars, blood stars, vermilion stars, sunflower stars, and rose stars. Purple sea urchins, green sea urchins, and California sea cucumbers are common. Limpets, lampshells, leafy hornmouths, and swimming scallops cling tenaciously to the rocks. Giant barnacles lie coated in orange encrusting sponge. Hermit crabs, galathaeid crabs, and red rock crabs move about the pinnacle. On the rocks, calcareous tube worms, terebellid worms, sea firs, white plumose anemones, and tealia anemones wave limbs and tentacles. In the sand, crimson anemones, tube-dwelling anemones, sea pens, and sea whips wave back.

Hutt Island Pinnacle is also a playground for fish. Lingcod, copper and tiger rockfish, shiner perch, grunt sculpins, sailfin sculpins, gobies, and eelpouts can be found. Divers who observe carefully can follow a trail of broken shells leading to an octopus in its den.

Looking south at the daymark from atop the pinnacle

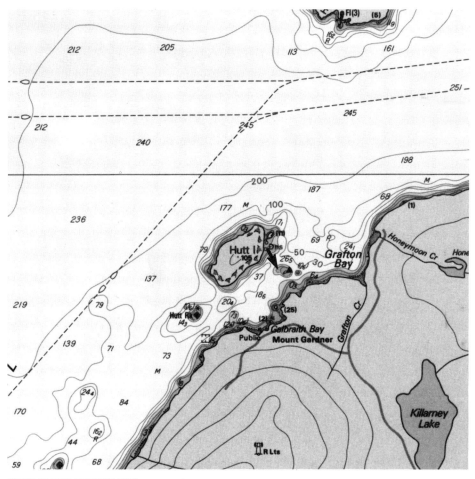

NOT TO BE USED FOR NAVIGATION—see page 9.
Use Canadian chart 3526 for navigation.
For information on obtaining navigational charts, see page 21.

147

162. Hutt Reef

Boat dive. . .rocky outcropping with mixed wall, reef, and sand bottom. . .marine life highlighted by wolf eels. . .hazards are boat traffic and current

Skill level   2 (see page 11)

Access   Boat dive

Location   Hutt Reef is between Hutt and Bowen Islands in south central Howe Sound. The reef is marked by a white and red triangular day marker on a cement base. Anchorage is available to the south of the marker in shallow water in fair holding ground. Anchorage can be difficult if a north or south wind is present. Descend the anchor line or at the reef and move around the reef.

Hazards   Boat traffic and current (see page 12)

Description   Hutt Reef provides a wide variety of geography and underwater life in one compact dive. The top of the reef, which dries on medium and low tides, provides interesting snorkelling as well as diving.

The north and west sides of the reef slope down 15 to 20 feet to a shell-covered sandy bottom. Large dendronotus rufus nudibranchs crawl about the array of broken scallop, clam, false Pacific jingle shell, mussel, and urchin shells. Sunflower stars and pink short-spined stars prowl about. Thousands of brittle stars scurrying about create an impression that the bottom is moving. Tube-dwelling anemones poke out of the sand and crushed shell. Large leafy brown kelp and green sea lettuce mix with mussels, barnacles, and purple sea stars in the shallower depths.

Move towards the southwest side of the reef and the bottom falls away. The dive becomes a wall dive to 50 or 60 feet. In this section, giant chimney sponges in only 50 feet of water grab the diver's attention. The wall is also home to sea peaches, hermit crabs, and lemon peel nudibranchs.

The wall continues around the south and along the eastern sections of the reef, although it shallows to 40 to 45 feet at its base. From there the bottom moves away in a gentle slope strewn with rocks and boulders. Large leafy brown kelp blankets some of the area. Boulders near the reef are covered in beautiful colonies of orange zoanthids.

Looking at the different sections of the reef, divers can expect to find whelks, clams, swimming scallops, leafy hornmouths, lined chitons, and the occasional gumboot chiton. Red rock, galathaeid, and hermit crabs scuttle about. Stalked hairy sea squirts, sea peaches, and orange finger sponge cling to the reef. Nudibranchs including alabaster, white, yellow margin, and lemon peel can be found on the rocks and the reef. Sea cucumbers stretch out along the bottom and up the wall of the reef. Striped sun stars, rose stars, painted stars, slime stars, blood stars, vermilion stars, and sunflower stars lie scattered everywhere. Painted tealia and plumose anemones wave their tentacles in search of food. Various fish, including rockfish, lingcod, sculpins, and greenlings, swim among the rocks. A possible highlight of the dive is seeing a wolf eel nestled in a crevice under a rock on the south side.

Looking south at the daymark

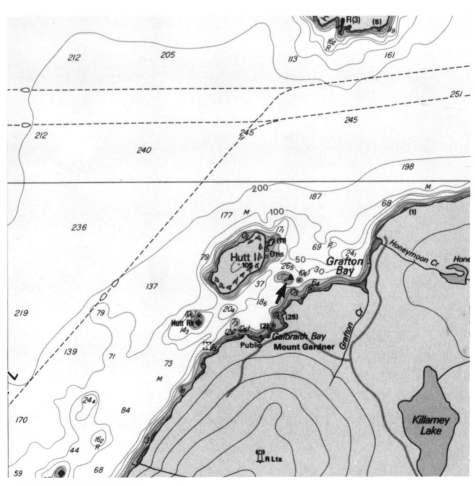

NOT TO BE USED FOR NAVIGATION—see page 9.
Use Canadian chart 3526 for navigation.
For information on obtaining navigational charts, see page 21.

149

163. Hutt Island South Wall

Boat dive. . . beginner wall dive with depths to 60 feet. . .good variety of life including hairy lithode and Puget Sound king crabs. . .hazard is boat traffic

Skill level 1 (see page 11)

Access Boat dive

Location Hutt Island is at the northwest tip of Bowen Island, 9 kilometres (5 nautical miles) from both Gibsons and Horseshoe Bay in south central Howe Sound. The wall takes up most of the south side of Hutt Island. It extends from the southeast tip of the island westward to a rocky outcropping 100 feet from the southwest tip. Anchorage is available near the southeast tip of the island. Descend and move west along the wall.

Hazards Boat traffic (see page 12)

Description The south side of Hutt Island is a great beginners' wall dive. It reaches depths of 35 to 60 feet before giving way to a steep sand bottom. The wall can be explored on one tank. The west tip of the island is a rocky point that is covered and uncovered by the tide. It provides some interesting snorkelling with lots of vegetation, mussels, barnacles, tidepool sculpins, small crabs, and schools of small fish. Mild current is sometimes found here.

The dive on the wall is quite rewarding. Purple stars, mussels, and barnacles inhabit the shallowest section. A bit deeper grow purple urchins, grey and green anemones, and calcareous tube worms. Along the wall, sea peaches and broad base tunicates mix with leafy hornmouths; sea cucumbers; and lemon peel, brown spotted, and yellow margin nudibranchs. Sea stars prowl the wall in search of food. Sunflower stars, painted stars, northern sunstars, morning sunstars, slime stars, and swimming scallops can all be seen. Fish school or swim by individually. Schools of striped perch, shiner perch, and pile perch swim just out of reach. Kelp greenlings, painted greenlings, and red Irish lords are solitary swimmers. The highlight of the dive is the crabs. We saw a hairy lithode crab and also a juvenile Puget Sound king crab that was just growing out of its orange colouring and starting to show the purple colours of an adult.

The south side seen from the south

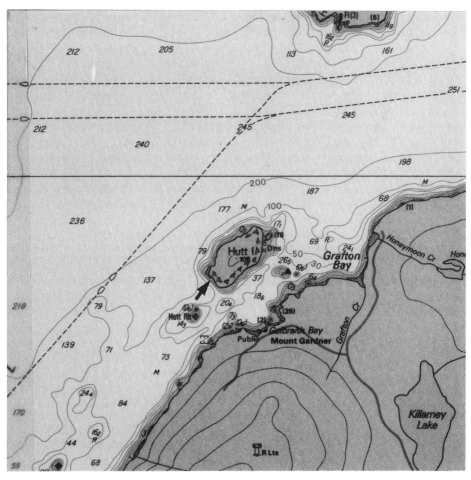

NOT TO BE USED FOR NAVIGATION—see page 9.
Use Canadian chart 3526 for navigation.
For information on obtaining navigational charts, see page 21.

151

164. Hutt Rock

Boat dive. . .mixed geography including wall, sand bottom, rocks, and boulders. . .very good selection of marine life. . .hazards are boat traffic and current

Skill level   1 or 2 (see page 11)

Access   Boat dive

Location   Hutt Rock is near the southeast tip of Hutt Island, 9 kilometres (5 nautical miles) from both Gibsons and Horseshoe Bay in south central Howe Sound. It is marked by a red and white diamond-shaped day marker on a cement base. Anchorage is available to the south of the marker in shallow water in good holding ground. Descend the anchor line and circle the rock.

Hazards   Boat traffic and current (see page 12)

Description   Hutt Rock is a dive with many faces. The south side of the rock slopes away from the marker and meets a boulder-strewn sand and shell bottom in 40 feet of water. To the west, the rock meets bottom in 15 to 20 feet, and the slope begins to steepen. Rounding the north side of the rock, the dive becomes a 55-foot wall dive with small cracks and crevices to explore. The crevices grow larger and the rock becomes craggy in the eastern section, finally giving way to the slope and boulders of the south.

The marine life at Hutt Rock varies with the geography. On the south side, a large colony of colourful zoanthids is packed onto a huge boulder. On the bottom, among rocks and broken shells, are sea pens; tube-dwelling anemones; orange, white, and grey plumose anemones; and brittle stars. Scattered on the slope of Hutt Rock are sunflower stars, pink short-spined stars, vermilion stars, whelks, and nudibranchs.

At the base of the western side, which is less boulder-strewn and only 15 to 20 feet deep, are large patches of leafy brown kelp. Among the kelp, green sea urchins, swimming and rock scallops, false Pacific jingle shells, and clam shells can be found. Purple stars inhabit the shallower waters. Large sea cucumbers and sunflower stars lie in about 20 feet, together with chitons, limpets, and the odd slime star. In the sand at the base of the rock are a toadfish, some sea pens, and some geoduck clams.

The north side of Hutt Rock has the largest variety of life. The sheer wall is home to sea peaches, orange sea cucumbers, glassy sea squirts, hermit crabs, and limpets. Swimming scallops covered in encrusting sponge cling to the wall. Kelp greenlings, lingcod, copper rockfish, and even a red Irish lord can be spotted. Two octopuses have set up dens in crevices near the base, along with some blood stars, painted stars, and pink mouthed hydroids. The end of the northern section is marked by a large crevice covered in brightly coloured zoanthids.

On the craggy east side are schools of quillback and copper rockfish as well as assorted stars.

The daymark marking the rock, with Hutt Island in the background

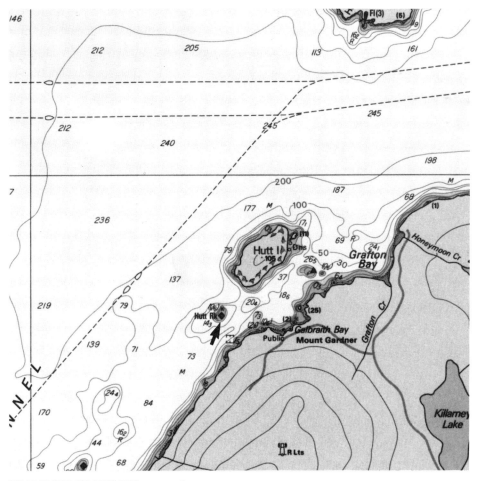

NOT TO BE USED FOR NAVIGATION—see page 9.
Use Canadian chart 3526 for navigation.
For information on obtaining navigational charts, see page 21.

153

165. Collingwood Channel Daymark

Boat dive. . . rocky reef can be circled on one tank . . . rocky outcroppings, sand/silt slopes, and tiered rock make up the bottom . . . large chimney sponge, anemones, and barnacles . . . hazards are boat traffic and current

Skill level 2 or 3 (see page 11)

Access Boat dive

Location Collingwood Channel Daymark is located between Bowen Island and Keats Island in south central Howe Sound. The daymark, which is on a cement base, marks a rocky reef that rises near the surface halfway between the north and south ends of the channel. The marker is a white diamond shape with a red triangle inside. Anchorage is best on the southwest side of the marker. Descend the anchor line and circle the reef.

Hazards Boat traffic and current (see page 12)

Description The marker rests on the shallowest part of a rocky reef which rises to a metre below the surface on very low tides. The reef can be circled on one tank. The top section is covered in kelp, sea lettuce, and rockweed. Some green urchins and purple stars and a large rusty towing cable are in this shallow section. Various shells are abundant. Triton, hornmouth, whelk, scallop, clam, and snail shells can be found. Some shells are home to their natural inhabitants, some to hermit crabs, and others lie empty.

The south and west sections of the reef descend to depths of 40 to 60 feet, where they meet a gently sloped sand and silt bottom. The highlight of this area is an enormous chimney sponge a metre high and half a metre wide. Brittle stars, long ray stars, crimson anemones, and tealia anemones inhabit this area. Barnacles covered in orange encrusting sponge cling to the reef.

As you move north, the terrain becomes rockier. One large boulder is packed with zoanthids. Lingcod and rockfish swim lazily or sit calmly observing divers. Blue top snails can also be found.

The east side provides a different look in geography and marine life. Two tiered sections descend to 70 feet, and then a steep slope goes into deeper water. Some deep ridges in the rock make for interesting viewing. Sea peaches, sunflower stars, chimney sponges, cloud sponges, shrimp, swimming scallops, white nudibranchs, alabaster nudibranchs, and warty tunicates are some of the marine life. An old, rotting fishing net lies along the bottom.

The daymark seen looking north up the channel

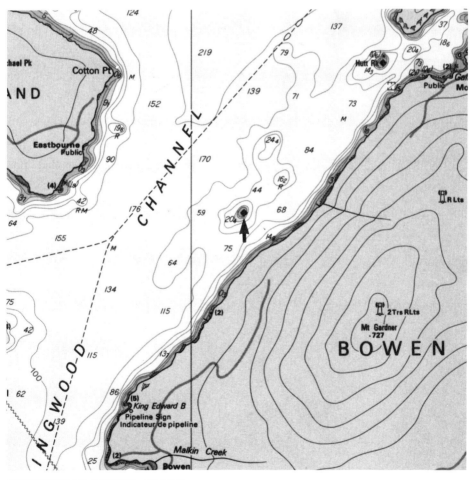

NOT TO BE USED FOR NAVIGATION—see page 9.
Use Canadian chart 3526 for navigation.
For information on obtaining navigational charts, see page 21.

155

166. Worlcombe Island

Boat dive. . .deep rock drop, deep and shallow sand slopes with rocky outcroppings, depths to 100 feet or more. . .great marine life, especially nudibranchs. . .hazards are current and depth

Skill level   2 or 3 (see page 11)

Access   Boat dive

Location   Worlcombe Island is 1.8 kilometres (1 nautical mile) west of Bowen Island in southwestern Howe Sound. The dive site is around the east tip of the island. A wooden triangle is fixed to a tree near the tip. Anchorage is available to the north or south of the site. Worlcombe Island is exposed to wind from all directions, so caution should be exercised when choosing an anchorage.

Hazards   Current and depth (see page 12)

Description   Worlcombe Island offers divers an intricate world of bottom types and marine life. The eastern tip of the island drops straight from the surface to 30 feet and then moves to 90 feet in a series of small ledges and walls. South of the tip, a gently sloped sand bottom is punctuated by rocks, boulders, small rock walls, and interesting ridged rocky outcroppings. Depths in this section can range from 20 to 100 or more feet.

Life at the point is packed onto the rock from top to bottom. Near the surface, leafy hornmouths, kelp greenlings, and painted stars live among the abundant vegetation. At 30 feet, zoanthid colonies cover the rock. Orange cup corals, striped perch, and copper rockfish also live at this level. Deeper still live calcareous tube worms, orange and tan cup corals, delicate cloud sponges, large chimney sponges, sea firs, light bulb tunicates, blood and slime stars, and clown shrimp.

South of the point, on the varied sand and rock bottom, divers find sea lemons, Nanaimo nudibranchs, white nudibranchs, janolus fuscus nudibranchs, dendronotus diversicolors, orange and white dendronotus rufus, tritonia festivas, and alabaster nudibranchs. Also in this area are sea pens, orange tennis ball sponges, lined chitons, Oregon hairy tritons, yellow boring sponge, warty tunicates, gumboot chitons, and red and purple sea urchins. An octopus lies curled up in its rocky den. Some large lingcod lie motionless on the bottom. Blackeye gobies retreat when divers approach.

The southeast side of the island with the triangular marker that marks the beginning of the dive

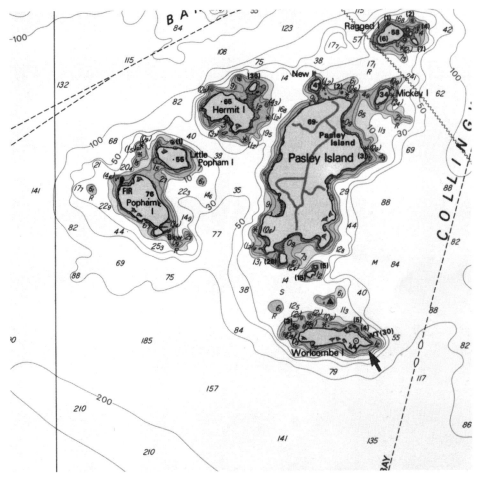

NOT TO BE USED FOR NAVIGATION—see page 9.
Use Canadian chart 3526 for navigation.
For information on obtaining navigational charts, see page 21.

157

167. Worlcombe Island Marker

Shallow reef, deepest on north side. . .thick vegetation on shallowest sections. . .craggy rock to explore. . .sand slope base. . .good mix of marine life including seals that swim with divers. . .hazards are current and wind

Skill level 1 (see page 11)

Access Boat dive

Location Worlcombe Island Marker is in the narrow channel between Worlcombe Island and Pasley Island in southern Howe Sound. The marker is a red and white triangle mounted on a cement base. It sits on top of a rock reef that is partly exposed on low tides. Anchorage is available north east of the marker in shallow water with good holding ground. Descend the anchor line and circle the reef.

Hazards Current and wind (see page 12)

Description Worlcombe Island Marker sits on a shallow reef in the quiet channel north of Worlcombe Island. The northern side of the reef slopes to 65 feet before meeting the sand. The other sides are relatively shallow, meeting the sand between 20 and 45 feet.

The rocky upper sections of the reef are home to beds of red and green sea lettuce, colonies of green sea urchins, patches of pink coralene algae, and clusters of purple stars. The craggy rock of the deeper sections hides many marine animals, while many others live out in the open. On a tour around the reef, divers can see leafy hornmouths, snails, umbrella crabs, decorator crabs, coonstripe shrimp, orange sea cucumbers, pink mouthed hydroids, painted tealia anemones, and yellow boring sponge. Giant barnacles push out purple legs in search of food.

Tiny fish such as scaleyhead sculpins, tidepool sculpins, and blackeye gobies scurry about the rocks. Larger fish such as kelp greenlings, lingcod, and copper and quillback rockfish swim slowly over the rock. Some enormous cabezons also live on the reef. Colourful opalescent and alabaster nudibranchs crawl slowly through the area. Rose stars, painted stars, and sunflower stars cling to rocks. In the sand around the reef live sea pens, pink short-spined stars, brittle stars, clams, and tube-dwelling anemones. Friendly seals live on the reef and sometimes join divers in the water.

The marker and cement base seen from the east

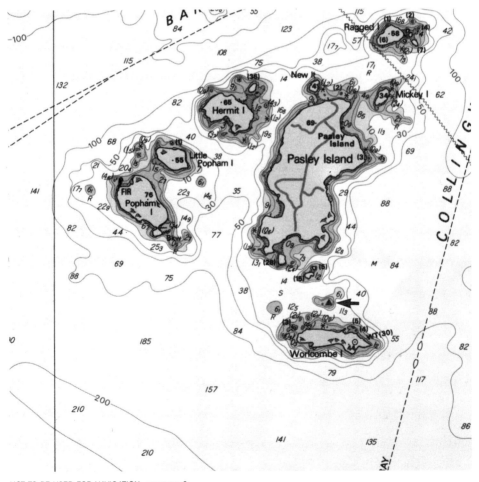

NOT TO BE USED FOR NAVIGATION—see page 9.
Use Canadian chart 3526 for navigation.
For information on obtaining navigational charts, see page 21.

159

168. Pasley South Islet

Varied depth and bottom depending on which side of islet you dive. . .deep wall south, shallower slope and flat bottom east and west, very shallow north. . .marine life varies with bottom. . .hazards are depth and current

Skill level   1, 2, or 3 (see page 11)

Access   Boat dive

Location   Pasley South Islet is directly south of Pasley Island, 2.8 kilometres (1.5 nautical miles) west of Bowen Island in southern Howe Sound. It is the horseshoe-shaped islet, the farther south of the two islets of Pasley Island. Anchorage is available in the shallow waters to the east and west of the islets. Dives can be conducted on all sides of the islet, depending on experience and training.

Hazards   Depth and current (see page 12)

Description   Pasley South Islet lends itself to dive groups of mixed abilities. The southern section is a straight drop into 100 feet or more of water. The east and west sections provide shallower water with gentle and medium slopes and rock piles. The northern part, a very shallow rock and sand mix, offers good snorkelling as well as shallow diving.

The steep drop on the southern islet is a smooth rock face with one spectacular large overhang. Intricate cloud sponge formations cover the area. Chimney sponges, lacy bryozoans, sea firs, glassy sea squirts, and tan cup corals live on the rock. Galathaeid crabs, decorator crabs, and decorated warbonnets live in the sponges. Also on the wall are hermit crabs, white nudibranchs, blood stars, swimming anemones, and red Irish lords.

The east and west sides of the islet slope upward as you move north. Some varied rock formations are home to many marine creatures. On the rocks are alabaster nudibranchs, painted stars, beds of small green urchins, false Pacific jingle shells, leafy hornmouths, and morning sunstars. In the sand around the rocks live sea pens, blackeye gobies, pink short-spined stars, and brittle stars. Schooling copper and quillback rockfish are everywhere. Large brooding cabezons stay close to the bottom and dart away when divers approach.

Shallow water at the northern end of the islet is a good place to snorkel or rest at a safety stop after a long dive. Some large pile perch and striped perch swim by in schools. Sea lettuce and kelp leaves cover small shells and miniature sunflower stars.

The islet seen from the south, with Pasley Island in the background

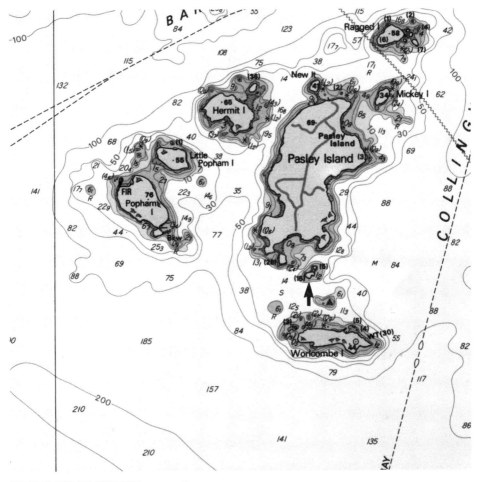

NOT TO BE USED FOR NAVIGATION—see page 9.
Use Canadian chart 3526 for navigation.
For information on obtaining navigational charts, see page 21.

161

169. Mickey Island Reef

Shallow reef with two rock fingers...depths to 65 feet...great life including wolf eels, octopus, Puget Sound king crabs, and large sea pens...hazards are boat traffic and current

Skill level   1 (see page 11)

Access   Boat dive

Location   Mickey Island is 1.8 kilometres (1 nautical mile) west of Bowen Island in southwestern Howe Sound. It is just off the northeast tip of Pasley Island. The dive site is the long narrow reef that extends from the southeast tip of the island. Anchorage is available on the reef or slightly north or south of it.

Hazards   Boat traffic and current (see page 12)

Description   Mickey Island extends two long rocky fingers into the water, providing a haven for a fantastic assortment of marine life. Depths run to 50 feet on the north finger and 65 feet on the south. In between and around the fingers is a gently sloped sand bottom. Average depth is about 35 feet.

The diverse life on and around the rocks includes some large sea pens, one 61 centimetres (24 inches) tall. Sea stars are represented by vermilion stars, slime stars, brittle stars, rose stars, blood stars, painted stars, and sunflower stars. The reef crawls with nudibranchs including yellow margin, alabaster, red, opalescent, sea lemon, and striped varieties. Fixed to the rock are cup corals, orange plumose anemones, crimson anemones, swimming anemones, and painted tealias.

In the deeper sections large chimney sponges provide hiding places for decorator crabs and shrimp. One boulder on the north finger in about 45 feet of water hosts a gathering of quillback rockfish. Close inspection reveals a pair of adult wolf eels cuddled up under the boulder.

Moving around the reef are more sea creatures, including a couple of octopus and Puget Sound king crabs. Leafy hornmouths, Oregon hairy tritons, swimming scallops, and green urchins all have small colonies. Sea firs wave in the water. Clinging to the rock are lacy bryozoans, warty tunicates, orange encrusting sponge, yellow boring sponge, coralene algae, and sea peaches. Orange cucumbers poke tentacles out into the open water, while their California cousins crawl slowly along the bottom. Fish life includes kelp greenlings, lingcod, and small sculpins.

The east side of the island; the dive is at the south end of the east side

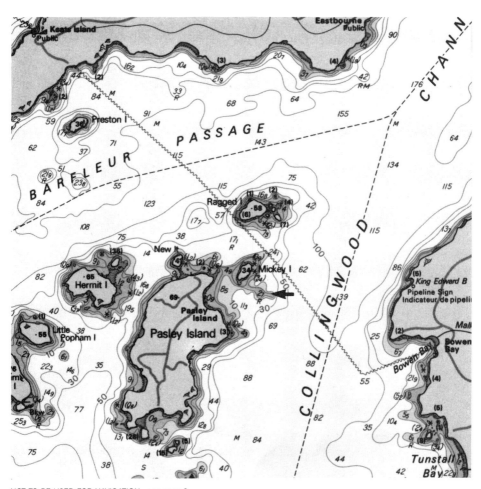

NOT TO BE USED FOR NAVIGATION—see page 9.
Use Canadian chart 3526 for navigation.
For information on obtaining navigational charts, see page 21.   163

170. Popham Island

Boat dive. . .shallow wall dive to 25 feet with gently sloped sand bottom at base and some rock and boulders in the sand. . .good variety of nudibranchs and other invertebrates . . .hazards are wind and current

Skill level   1 (see page 11)

Access   Boat dive

Location   Popham Island is 3.7 kilometres (2 nautical miles) south east of Gibsons in southwestern Howe Sound. The dive site is along the southern section of the island. Anchorage is available south of the island or south of the large stone breakwater that extends from the southeast corner of the island. Caution should be exercised when anchoring, as this area is exposed to winds from the Strait of Georgia.

Hazards   Wind and current (see page 12)

Description   A shallow wall, a gently sloping sand bottom, and abundant marine life make Popham Island an easy and fun dive. The south end of the island is a wall that drops down to a sand bottom at 25 feet maximum. The sand bottom's gradual slope allows divers to pick the depth they wish to explore. Occasional boulder and rock outcroppings, mostly on the western section of the site, provide habitat for sea life.

The wall face at Popham is a colourful place. Blood stars and purple stars gather in clusters. Leather stars, ochre stars, sunflower stars, and painted stars also hang off the wall. Giant barnacles covered in orange encrusting sponge, rainbow-coloured lined chitons, and brown gumboot chitons cling to the rock. Leafy hornmouths are abundant. Divers also find sea peaches; California cucumbers; and alabaster, white, and yellow margin nudibranchs. Swimming just off the wall are schooling shiner perch, large pile perch, and kelp greenlings.

The boulders at the base of the wall provide homes for mussel and barnacle colonies. Groups of lightbulb tunicates, orange tennis ball sponges, Pacific pink scallops, and green sea urchins cluster around the rocks. On the sandy slope live various nudibranchs including dendronotus rufus, janolus fuscus, striped and opalescent. Crimson anemones and sea firs also live in this area. Buried in the sand are geoduck clams. Red rock crabs and many flatfish lie on the sand. Some very large lingcod lie motionless on the bottom. The stone breakwater provides hiding spots for marine life and will be worth watching in future years to see what may develop along its face.

The south side of the island, with the breakwater on the right

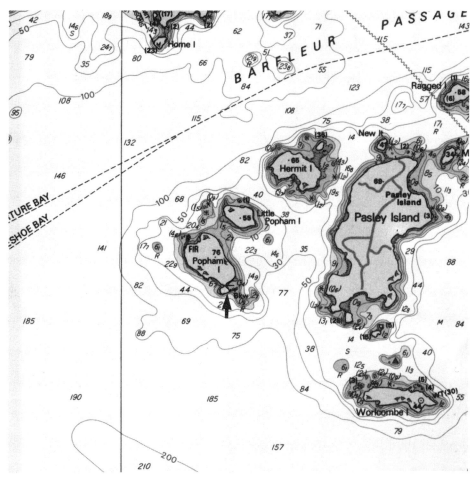

NOT TO BE USED FOR NAVIGATION—see page 9.
Use Canadian chart 3526 for navigation.
For information on obtaining navigational charts, see page 21.

165

171. Preston Island

Simple shallow dive on rock slope, with sand slope descending past 100 feet . . . interesting rock formations to west of island . . . good mix of marine life in all sections . . . hazards are wind and boat traffic

Skill level   1 (see page 11)

Access   Boat dive

Location   Preston Island is 2.7 kilometres (1.4 nautical miles) east of Gibsons in southwestern Howe Sound. The dive site is the southern part of the island. Anchorage is available on the east and south sides of the island. Care should be exercised when choosing an anchorage, as this area is open to winds from the south.

Hazards   Wind and boat traffic (see page 12)

Description   Preston Island is a shallow, simple dive typical of the diving in the southwest section of Howe Sound. The rocky slope of the island continues underwater, where it meets the bottom in 15 to 25 feet of water. A gentle sand slope that is strewn, particularly on the west side, with rocks and boulders moves away from the island to depths of 100 feet or more. Most of the marine life is in 35 feet or less.

The large boulders and jagged rock slabs of Preston Island's west side provide hiding spots and habitat for marine life and an interesting landscape for divers to view. Many types of rockfish, including copper, quillback, and tiger, can be found among the rocks. Other life in the shallow sections includes leather stars, sunflower stars, short-spined stars, mottled slime stars, orange sea cucumbers, white and grey plumose anemones, painted tealia anemones, broad base squirts, sea peaches, and wrinkled squirts. Alabaster nudibranchs, yellow margin nudibranchs, flabellina salmonacea, and sea lemons are found in the area. Beds of green urchins lie in shallow water alongside sea lettuce, kelp, and rockweed. Shelled animals include leafy hornmouths, tritons, blue top snails, lined chitons, false Pacific jingle shells, and Pacific pink scallops.

A quick look around the deep sections of Preston Island turns up some interesting life. Sea firs, lacy bryozoans, and crimson anemones wave through the water. Scattered on the bottom are sea pens, white plumose anemones, rose stars, lampshells, and white cucumbers. Scuttling about the sand are brittle stars and hermit crabs.

The island seen from the southwest, with Keats Island in the background

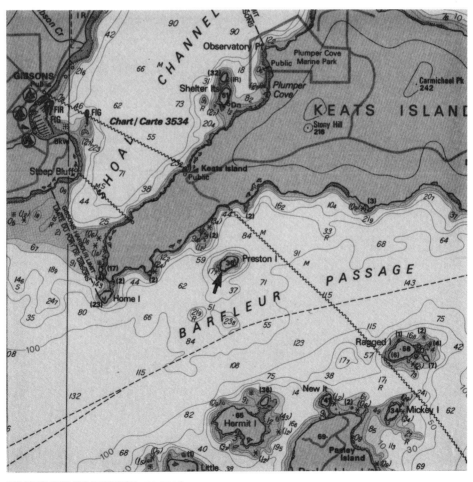

NOT TO BE USED FOR NAVIGATION—see page 9.
Use Canadian chart 3526 for navigation.
For information on obtaining navigational charts, see page 21.

167

172. Halkett Wall

Boat dive...wall with depths down to 100 feet or more before steep sand bottom takes over...rows of invertebrate life including plumose anemones, cloud and chimney sponges, and sea peaches...hazards are depth and boat traffic

Skill level 3 (see page 11)

Access Boat dive

Location Halkett Wall is on the southeastern tip of Gambier Island, 8.3 kilometres (4.6 nautical miles) north of Horseshoe Bay in central Howe Sound. To find the site, move northeast from the southernmost tip of Halkett Point for 400 metres. Look for two rocks showing slightly above the surface. The wall is just north of the rocks and is marked above water by a series of large white stains on the rock. Anchorage is impossible at this site, so a tended boat is needed. Enter north of the two rocks and move north.

Hazards Depth and boat traffic (see page 12)

Description Halkett Wall is laid out like a garden with invertebrate life arranged in rows. The dive is a sheer wall that runs over a short distance on a north/south line. Depths plummet to 100 feet or more along the wall before it gives way to a steep sand bottom. The northern end has a small ledge in 30 feet of water. Numerous crevices, some quite deep into the rock, give places for marine life to hide.

The rows of invertebrates are in deep and shallow water along Halkett Wall. In deep water, cloud sponges and chimney sponges grow. Green and red shrimp, prawns, and galatheaid crabs crawl like garden insects among the sponges. The deep sand slope has bunches of tube-dwelling anemones. Move a bit shallower and the wall is packed with curly white calcareous tube worms. On the rock are beds of sea peaches, zoanthids, yellow boring sponge, and plumose anemones. Small groups of orange cup corals are spread throughout the site. At the shallowest depths, purple stars, looking somewhat overplanted, cluster together in tightly packed groups. Rose stars and sunflower stars may be seen. Painted brittle stars wave the tips of their arms from inside crevices in the rock. Common brown brittle stars lie by the hundreds on top of the sand and crawl away if disturbed.

Vertebrate life also clusters around Halkett Wall. Red Irish lords and painted greenlings lie camouflaged on the rock. Lingcod and kelp greenlings watch warily and flee when divers approach. Tiger rockfish and copper rockfish are wedged in crevices. Schools of striped perch swim about the top 20 feet of the wall.

The wall seen from the east

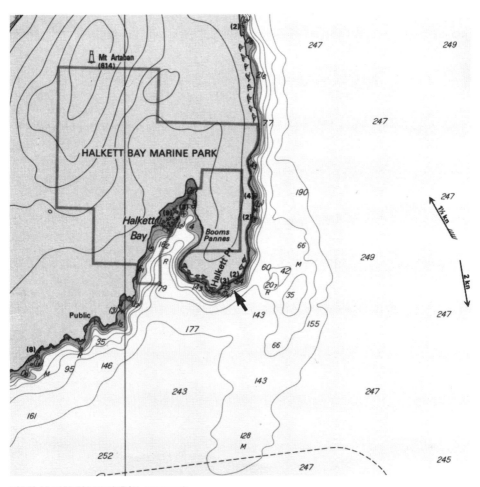

NOT TO BE USED FOR NAVIGATION—see page 9.
Use Canadian chart 3526 for navigation.
For information on obtaining navigational charts, see page 21.

169

173. Gambier Island East Wall

Boat dive. . .deep wall and shallow wall on one site with sloped sand ledge between. . . deep and shallow life. . .hazards are depth and boat traffic

Skill level   2 or 3 (see page 11)

Access   Boat dive

Location   Gambier Island East Wall is located 9.7 kilometres (5.4 nautical miles) north of Horseshoe Bay in the centre of Howe Sound. The site is a 1-kilometre-long (.8 nautical mile) series of cliffs 1.8 kilometres (1 nautical mile) north of Halkett Point on the southeast side of Gambier Island. Dives can be conducted from the north or south end. Anchorage is difficult except at the north end of the cliffs, where a sandy ledge has holding ground for small vessels. A tended boat is advised, especially if any wind is present. Descend and follow the wall.

Hazards   Depth and boat traffic (see page 12)

Description   Dive either a shallow wall or a deep wall on Gambier's east side. Both are available at this site. The shallow wall runs from the surface to about 35 feet. A sloping ledge takes over and moves eastward and deeper to a depth of 45 to 55 feet. The second wall then moves down to 100 feet or more.

The top of the shallow wall is packed with acorn barnacles, mussels, purple stars, and leather stars. Schooling striped perch and shiner perch move about close to the wall. An octopus, green sea urchins, California sea cucumbers, sunflower stars, pink short-spined stars, and tube-dwelling anemones inhabit the sandy ledge between the walls.

The deep wall is home to slippered cucumbers, white cucumbers, orange cucumbers, cloud and chimney sponges, and false Pacific jingle shells. Colonies of calcareous tube worms cover sections of rock. Sea peaches, broad base sea squirts, and glassy sea squirts also appear. Groups of a mysterious balloon-shaped white tunicate live just under the lip of small rocky overhangs. Red and white blood stars, painted stars, spiny stars, striped sun stars, and sunflower stars cling to the wall. Swimming scallops fly through the water when disturbed. Quillback rockfish hide in cracks, while lingcod stare placidly into the water before them. Yellow boring sponge, encrusting sponges, and encrusting bryozoans add colour to the site.

The south end of the wall seen from the south

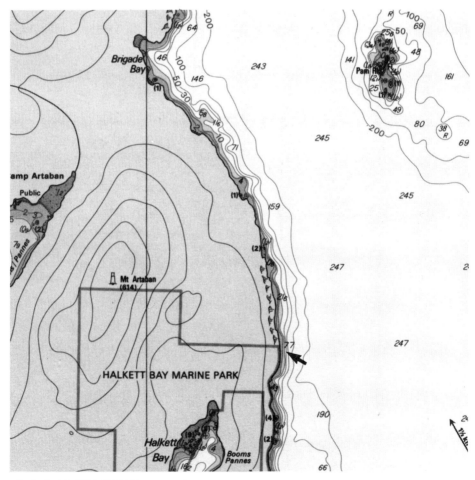

NOT TO BE USED FOR NAVIGATION—see page 9.
Use Canadian chart 3526 for navigation.
For information on obtaining navigational charts, see page 21.

171

174. Brigade Bay North Wall

Boat dive. . .vertical drop with one ledge at 25 to 35 feet and depths past 100 beyond the ledge. . .out-of-the-ordinary marine life including skates, hairy lithode crabs, and sharks. . .hazard is depth

Skill level   3 (see page 11)

Access   Boat dive

Location   Brigade Bay North Wall is 13.9 kilometres (8 nautical miles) north of Horseshoe Bay on the east side of Gambier Island in central Howe Sound. The dive site runs along the cliffs north of the northern tip of Brigade Bay. Anchorage is available at the northern and southern ends of the cliffs, but the bottom's steep slope makes anchorage difficult on windy days. A tended boat is recommended when the weather is windy.

Hazards   Depth (see page 12)

Description   The wall north of Brigade Bay is a deep dive, where you see some creatures not found on everyday dives. A vertical drop, interrupted by one ledge in 25 to 35 feet of water, moves well beyond the range of sport diving before bottoming out. Most of the interesting life is at 50 or more feet, hidden or partly hidden in the cracks and crevices in the wall.

A careful search of the north wall reveals many interesting marine animals, including hairy lithode crabs, galathaeid crabs, and lampshells. Giant barnacles lie covered in orange encrusting sponge. Decorator crabs are well hidden among the rocks and plants. Orange cup corals stand out on rocks. Crimson anemones, orange swimming anemones, and orange and white plumose anemones add their colour to the wall. Calcareous tube worms coat some rocks. Cloud sponges start in 65 feet and are seen frequently. False Pacific jingle shells are glued to the wall. Sea pens can sometimes be seen. An octopus lives in one of the few boulder piles. Lingcod also frequent the deeper water.

The shallow waters, above 50 feet, have some interesting life. Orange and slippered sea cucumbers are wedged between or under rocks on the ledge. Large California cucumbers lie about. Stalked hairy sea squirts and brown spotted nudibranchs provide colour. Sunflower and painted stars prowl the shallow wall. A large skate greeted us at the north end of the wall, as did a creature that suspiciously resembled a six-gill shark. Neither was very friendly. The shark swam a circle around the two of us before heading away. A smaller, more docile buffalo sculpin was also in the shallow water.

Divers with air and time left over should tuck inside the bay to the north of the wall. Here they find every size and colour of sunflower star among the thousands pasted all over the rocks.

The north point seen from the south

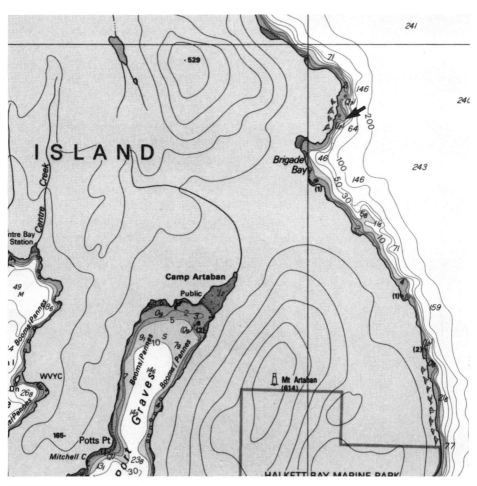

NOT TO BE USED FOR NAVIGATION—see page 9.
Use Canadian chart 3526 for navigation.
For information on obtaining navigational charts, see page 21.

173

175. Ekins Point

Boat dive. . .depths to 100 feet to the west and north, gentler slope to the north . . .good variety of life and interesting rolling hills. . .hazards are boat traffic and depth

Skill level   1, 2, or 3 (see page 11)

Access   Boat dive

Location   Ekins Point, the north tip of Gambier Island, is 19.7 kilometres (10.9 nautical miles) north of Horseshoe Bay in north central Howe Sound. It is marked by a white circular tower with a white light that flashes after dusk. Anchorage is available directly north of the marker. Descend at the marker or to the east or west and explore the area around the point.

Hazards   Boat traffic and depth (see page 12)

Description   Ekins Point has rolling hills and deep and shallow attractions. The rock north of the marker forms a series of smooth, rounded underwater hills between 25 and 40 feet deep before dropping sharply into deeper water. On the east and west sides of the point, steep drops with rolling ledges move past 100 feet very quickly. All areas are covered by a fine coating of silt.

The deep sections to the west of the point are strewn with typical deep-water life. Large flowing crimson anemones and tiny stiff cup corals are on the bottom. Some walls are covered in calcareous tube worms with their white coiled tubes and coloured tentacles. Black and grey long ray stars stretch out over the rock. Lampshells with characteristic rippled shells hang off the wall. Dendronotus diversicolor nudibranchs with fiery red cerata dot the landscape. A mystery of sorts presents itself in the form of rows of dead cloud sponges that are brown and decaying but still cling to the rock and provide homes for galathaeid crabs.

In the shallower rolling hills north of the point, another selection of marine life is arrayed. Zoanthid colonies cover some rocks, while clumps of orange and white plumose anemones stand tree-like on others. Patches of thatched barnacles, some overgrown with orange encrusting sponge, cling to the bottom. Also in this area are green urchins, purple urchins, blood stars, painted stars, vermilion stars, and swimming anemones. The shallowest sections are thick with Oregon hairy tritons and whelks. Moving about the site are shrimp, kelp greenlings, and rockfish.

The point seen from the west

NOT TO BE USED FOR NAVIGATION—see page 9.
Use Canadian chart 3526 for navigation.
For information on obtaining navigational charts, see page 21.

175

176. Hope Point

Boat dive. . .varied bottom includes rocky reef, sloped sand, and small wall. . .vegetation and California cucumbers drape the reef. . .tube-dwelling anemones in sand and octopus and fish around wall. . .depths to 90 feet at reef base, shallower on wall. . .hazards are boat traffic and wind

Skill level   1, 2, or 3 (see page 11)

Access   Boat dive

Location   Hope Point is 10.1 kilometres (5.4 nautical miles) northwest of Horseshoe Bay on southeast Gambier Island in central Howe Sound. The point is at the south end of the large finger of land west of Halkett Point on southern Gambier. It is marked by a white circular tower with a white light that flashes after dusk. Anchorage is available south of the marker. Descend the anchor line and move east.

Hazards   Boat traffic and wind (see page 12)

Description   Hope Point is an easy dive with three different bottom types and a good variety of life. A rocky reef extends south of the marker into 80 feet of water. To the east, a sand and silt bottom slopes away. Farther east, a shallow wall runs deeper than 35 feet. Each area has its own distinctive life.

The rocky reef looks like a salad bowl of brown broad-leaf kelp and red and green sea lettuce. Striped perch and shiner perch school by the thousands. On the reef, ledges covered in silt and shell are home to California cucumbers, purple stars, red rock crabs, and coralene algae. Careful searches through the kelp reveal lobefin snailfish and scaleyhead sculpins. The sandy bottom at the base of the reef and to the east is covered by tube-dwelling anemones, pink short-spined stars, sunflower stars, and heart cockles. A stray rock outcropping in 50 feet of water is covered by large orange and white plumose anemones.

The shallow wall with its rock-strewn sand bottom is home to an octopus, sailfin sculpins, orange cup corals, yellow boring sponge and starfish including sunflower stars and slime stars. Divers can explore little cracks and crevices and find coonstripe shrimp and other life.

Hope Point provides variety in life and scenery. There is a small community in the bay near the point, and residents take a dim view of divers pillaging the bottom.

The marker and east wall seen from the southwest

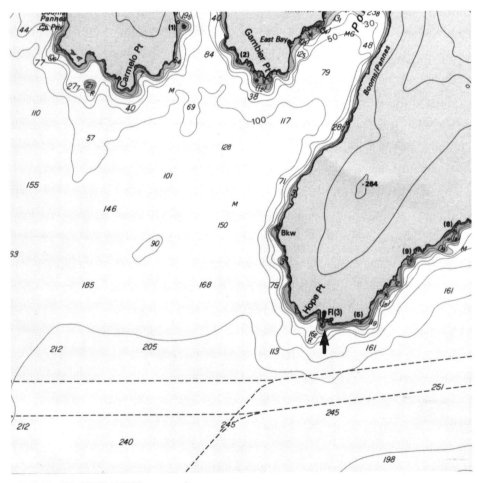

177. Carmelo Point

Boat dive. . .shallow dive over large area. . .bottom rock and mud/sand mix to depths of 50 feet. . .many shelled creatures and nudibranchs. . .some bottles and vases. . . hazard is boat traffic

Skill level   1 (see page 11)

Access   Boat dive

Location   Carmelo Point is 9.6 kilometres (5.3 nautical miles) northeast of Gibsons on southern Gambier Island in central Howe Sound. It is wedged between West Bay and Centre Bay on the second finger of land from the west side of Gambier. Anchorage is available in shallow water with good holding ground to the east of the point in a small bay. Descend on the west side of the bay and follow the point south and west.

Hazards   Boat traffic (see page 12)

Description   Carmelo Point offers a diverse world spread out over a large area. The rocky shore drops down to 15 to 35 feet and then gives way to a gently sloped mud and sand bottom punctuated by rocky outcroppings. Each different bottom type has its own life and points of interest. Depths along the sloped sections run 25 to 50 feet; deep water is quite a swim away.

In the sand and mud areas of the dive, some interesting bottles and vases lie partly buried. The southeastern tip of the point is particularly good for finding odd-shaped and odd-sized items. Marine life in the area includes orange sea pens, purple and grey tube-dwelling anemones, red rock crabs, pink short-spined stars, white moon snails, and red and white dendronotus rufus nudibranchs. On the rocky outcroppings are orange and white plumose anemones, stalked hairy sea squirts, broad base squirts, leather stars, ochre stars, painted stars, orange finger sponge, false Pacific jingle shells, and alabaster nudibranchs.

The rocky area descending from the shore combines much of the life found on the rocky outcroppings and some creatures unique to its own space. Here you find blood stars, morning sunstars, green sea urchins, tritons, whelks, mudflat snails, and leafy hornmouths. Opalescent and hooded nudibranchs grow on kelp leaves. Dungeness crabs, buffalo sculpins, and mottled sole hide camouflaged on the rock.

The east side of the point—note the wooden bench on shore

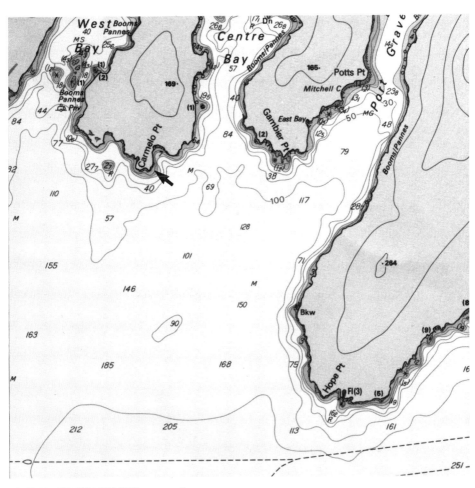

178. Grace Islet Rock

Boat dive. . .shallow, compact patch dive. . .60-foot maximum depth. . .large variety of marine life including nudibranchs, sea stars, cucumbers, urchins, and fish. . .hazards are boat traffic and wind

Skill level   1 (see page 11)

Access   Boat dive

Location   Grace Islet is on the southwest tip of Gambier Island, 5.2 kilometres (2.9 nautical miles) north of Gibsons in southwestern Howe Sound. The dive site is the submerged rock 100 metres directly south of the more western of the two islets. The islet is marked by a white circular tower with a white light that flashes after dusk. Anchorage is available in the sand bottom in 30 to 40 feet of water to the south of the marker. Caution should be exercised when anchoring to avoid hitting the rock or swinging into it while at anchor. Descend the anchor line and explore the area.

Hazards   Boat traffic and wind (see page 12)

Description   Grace Islet Rock is a compact dive, easy to find and easy to explore. The top of the rock is awash on very low tides. The rock descends to 45 feet on the west side, 60 feet on the south, and 30 on the east. At the base is a gently sloped sand bottom sprinkled with logs and cables. Small walls, crevices, rocky ridges, and miniature valleys give ample ground for exploration.

A circuit of Grace Islet Rock is a relaxing patch dive that rewards the diver with a great variety of marine life. The sandy slope at the base of the rock is alive with brittle stars, shrimp, and tube-dwelling anemones. Purple and red sea urchins can be seen. False Pacific jingle shells, acorn barnacles, gumboot chitons, pale blue chitons, and yellow boring sponge adhere to the rock.

While exploring the rock, you also find broad base sea squirts, stalked hairy sea squirts, sea peaches, blood stars, vermilion stars, morning sunstars, and sunflower stars. Nudibranchs including yellow margin, opalescent, alabaster, hooded, sea lemon, and dendronotus rufus inhabit the area. Shelled creatures are represented by swimming scallops, tritons, leafy hornmouths, moon snails, dungeness crabs, and heart crabs. California sea cucumbers, slippered cucumbers, and orange cucumbers are at various depths. Lingcod, kelp greenlings, copper rockfish, and blackeye gobies also inhabit the area. The shallower waters at the top of the rock are home to sea lettuce, algae, kelp, green urchins, and purple stars.

The tower at the southwest side of the islet

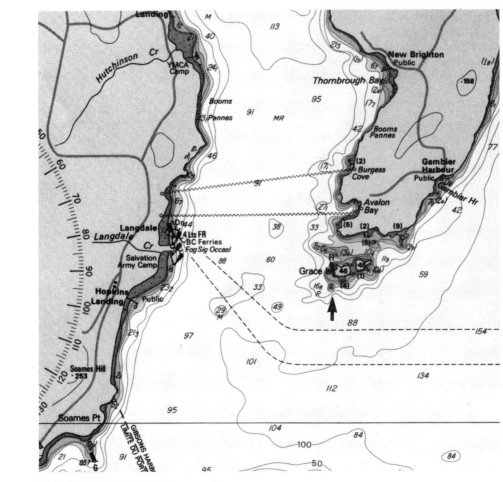

NOT TO BE USED FOR NAVIGATION—see page 9.
Use Canadian chart 3526 for navigation.
For information on obtaining navigational charts, see page 21.

181

179. **Mariners Rest** (also called Steamboat Rock)

Varied bottom in a compact site. . .deep sections including walls west and north . . .shallow sand east and south. . .good number of nudibranchs and good mix of other life. . .hazards are boat traffic, depth, and current

Skill level 2 or 3 (see page 11)

Access Boat dive

Location Mariners Rest is 4.7 kilometres (2.5 nautical miles) north of the Langdale ferry terminal in western Howe Sound. The dive site rings the large rock topped by a white wooden cross on the west side of Gambier Island. The area is used as a last resting place for the ashes of sailors who wish their remains to be given up to the sea. Anchorage is available to the south of the rock or between the rock and Gambier. Descend and circle the rock.

Hazards Boat traffic, depth, and current (see page 12)

Description Mariners Rest is a compact site in which to observe the sea creatures that live on different bottom types. The north and west sides are steep rocky drops and wall faces running from the surface to well beyond 100 feet. On the east and south sides, shallow sand slopes with some rocks and boulders lie between 15 and 50 feet deep.

Mariners Rest and Gambier Island are separated by a narrow trench with a sand bottom 30 to 40 feet deep. Diving in this area, you may be visited by dogfish and pile perch and can observe sea pens, tube-dwelling anemones, orange plumose anemones, dendronotus rufus, and a gigantic log covered by sunflower stars.

As you move north and west, the steep rocky bottom holds beds of green sea urchins, walls of calcareous tube worms, and colonies of orange zoanthids. False Pacific jingle shells, wrinkled stars and white plumose anemones adhere to the rock. Tall logs, evidence of nearby logging and pulp mills, hang at weird angles from deep ledges on the wall face. Glued to the rock are lampshells, swimming scallops, thatched barnacles, tan cup corals, yellow boring sponge, orange finger sponge, white nudibranchs, and purple urchins.

The rock-strewn, gently sloped sand of the south side of Mariners Rest has its own collection of life. Giant nudibranchs with bright orange-tipped cerata dance when lifted up in the water. Orange nudibranchs, green urchins, glassy sea squirts, and an octopus live around the rocks. In the sand, short-spined, painted, and brittle stars crawl about. Divers with a quick eye can glimpse slime feather dusters before they withdraw into their jellylike structures.

Mariners Rest seen from the south

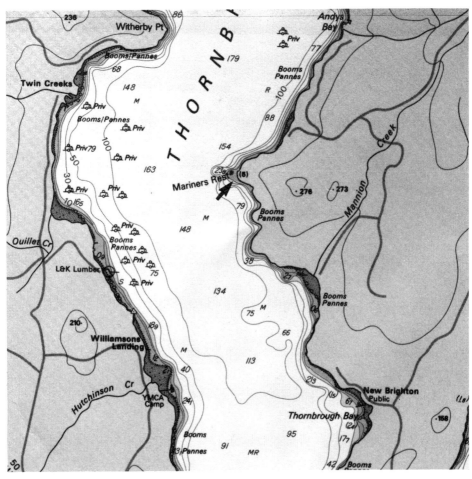

NOT TO BE USED FOR NAVIGATION—see page 9.
Use Canadian chart 3526 for navigation.
For information on obtaining navigational charts, see page 21.

183

180. Soames Point

Boat dive close to Gibsons. . .very gently sloped bottom of sand, rock, and boulder to 60 feet. . .great beginner boat dive. . .good variety of life, with some bottles and plates as well. . .hazards are boat traffic and current

Skill level 1 (see page 11)

Access Boat dive

Location Soames Point is 1.8 kilometres (1 nautical mile) north of Gibsons in southwestern Howe Sound. It is marked by a green spar buoy marked Q57. Anchorage is available on the northeast or southeast side of the buoy. Descend the anchor line or the mooring line on the buoy and explore the area.

Hazards Boat traffic and current (see page 12)

Description Soames Point is a very good first boat dive, especially for those in the Gibsons area. The bottom is a gentle, almost imperceptibly sloped boulder-strewn sand plain reaching depths of 50 to 60 feet west of the spar buoy. The rocks begin to thin out as you reach 50 feet, and a few small ledges and drops appear. Divers can explore this site without fear of kicking up a lot of silt or tumbling off a ledge into deep water. The chain holding the buoy provides a descent/ascent line and reference point.

Soames Point is also a good place to sharpen skills as a marine life observer. Some of the life is out in the open, while some is hidden or partly hidden by the rocks. In the open are patches of pink coralene algae, colonies of yellow boring sponge, and groups of white and orange plumose anemones. Alabaster nudibranchs, leather stars, and sunflower stars move slowly across the bottom. Green sea urchins lie in small beds on top of boulders. Hermit crabs race around the rocks in their acquired houses. Swimming scallops fly up, looking like living false teeth if divers tap their shells.

Buffalo sculpins, red rock crabs, and dungeness crabs are partly hidden and blend in with the bottom. Hiding under and among the rocks are quillback rockfish, gobies, and octopus. Interesting man-made objects such as old plates and bottles lie scattered about the bottom.

The green spar buoy at the point

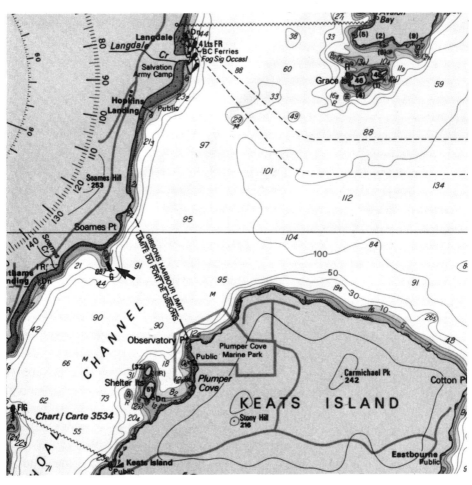

A Selection of Books Published by Gordon Soules Book Publishers

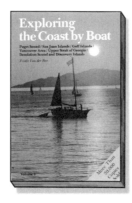

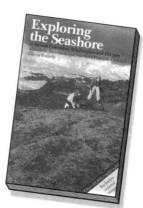

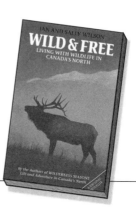